THE NEW
Women of Color
DAILY DEVOTIONAL

The New Women of Color Daily Devotional

The articles and prayers are taken from the *Women of Color Devotional Bible* © World Bible / Nia Publishing Co.

Urban Spirit! Publishing and Media Company is an African American owned company based in Atlanta, GA. You can find more information at http://www.urbanspirit.biz/

The New Women of Color Daily Devotional Fall/Winter Edition © Urban Spirit! Publishing and Media Company)

Produced with the assistance of Cheryl Wilson, i4Details and Larry Taylor, LTD2

All Scripture quotes, unless otherwise indicated, are from the Authorized King James Version of the Bible.

Scripture quotes marked Amplified are from the Amplified Bible, © Copyright 1954, 1958, 1962, 1964, 1965, 1987 by The Lockman Foundation.

Scripture quotes marked NASB are taken from the New American Standard Bible® Copyright © 1960, 1962, 1963, 1968, 1971, 1972, 1973, 1975, 1977, 1995 by The Lockman Foundation.

Scripture quotes marked NIV are taken from the HOLY BIBLE, NEW INTERNATIONAL VERSION®. Copyright© 1973, 1978, 1984 by the International Bible Society.

Scripture quotes marked NLT are taken from the Holy Bible, New Living Translation, copyright © 1996. Used by permission of Tyndale House Publishers, Inc, Wheaton, Illinois 60189. All rights reserved.

Manufactured in the United States of America

THE NEW
Women of Color
DAILY DEVOTIONAL

FALL/WINTER EDITION

To: Keona
Thanks for being there,
especially when I didn't think I would make it!

M

SEPTEMBER

WEEK ONE: DEPENDENCY ON GOD

DAY 1 / THE DIVINE VINE

GET CONNECTED TO THE SOURCE...

"I am the vine, ye are the branches: he that abideth in me, and I in him, the same bringeth forth much fruit: for without me you can do nothing."
John 15:5

When I go to a quiet place and close myself in to commune with God, I often bring my portable CD player. After a couple of hours the CD player stops. I press Play; the CD starts at the beginning again, and then stops. That's how batteries work. They are limited and you can only rely on their power for a while. I've found that using an adapter to connect my CD player to an electrical outlet is a better option. The outlet provides continuous power that will only stop if there's a power outage or the electric bill is neglected. So it is—in an even deeper, eternally reliable manner—with the sap from the true vine, the source of life flowing from Jesus to us.

APPLICATION

Sweet is the sap that flows from the vine to the branches, bringing life. The vine depends on the gardener's knowledge and experience, and the branch depends for its nourishment on the vine and the continuous flow of sap. In the same way, we are the branches and are dependent on Jesus, the true vine. The gardener is our Father God. Jesus calls us to remain in Him and depend on Him. A continuous connection to the vine is imperative for our spiritual life. In John 15:5, Jesus tells us, "Abide in me, for without me you can do nothing." Everyone is dependent on a loving God.

Draw a line down the center of a sheet of paper. On one side, list items that show your strength and self-sufficiency in the natural world, such as your salary, purchases of clothing, the most recent meal you paid for at a restaurant, etc. Now ask yourself: What comprises my dependency on God? On the other side of the paper, list examples of your dependency on God, such as spiritual nurture, inner strength, salvation—anything that you believe deeply about. Draw lines that connect the items on both sides to a sentence at the bottom of the page. Begin the sentence with an affirmation: I am dependent on God because_____. Display the paper in a prominent spot in your home.

PRAYER

Jesus, in the depths of my heart, I need to capture the truth of my vital connection to You. Free me from thinking that I can make it without You. Let me see the reality of my need for You in all things, at all times. In Your name, I pray. Amen.

DAY 2 / ONENESS

WITH CHRIST...

"That they all may be one; as thou, Father, art in me, and I in thee...."
John 17:21a

After 19 years together, my husband and I have developed a remarkable sensitivity to each other. Without speaking a word, we communicate our needs and how to meet them. This oneness and unity strengthens our relationship, as well as strengthening us individually. I am so lucky to have my husband in my life. He is all I need and I am all he needs to make it in today's world.

APPLICATION

Being dependent on someone else is often mistakenly seen as a sign of weakness, especially by modern women. Conversely, having a successful relationship is often mistakenly seen as requiring only mutual love and care for one another. But leaving God out of the picture of a so-called "successful" relationship or trusting in our own strength rather than in God puts us on dangerous ground. Independence from God is a deception of the world that will destroy our relationship with Christ. Oneness with Him is our destiny. Jesus longed for us to depend on Him the way He depended on His Father (John 17:21). A couple that recognizes their need for dependency on God as their primary source of nurturing and strength will then seek ways to show this awareness in their relationship.

Practice being dependent on Christ. Start with a few small things. For instance, as you begin your day, ask Jesus what you should wear or what route you should take to work or school. Get into the habit of depending on Him in everything. Notice how this habitual dependency on God unfolds in your relationships with people you care about.

PRAYER

Lord, I am undisciplined in depending on You. Help me to break the bondage of independence and come to depend on You in all things. In Jesus' name, I pray. Amen.

DAY 3 / S.O.S. SEEKING OUR SAVIOR

SEND OUT A DISTRESS CALL TODAY...

*"In my distress, I called upon the Lord, and cried unto my God:
he heard my voice out of his temple, and my cry came before him,
even unto his ears."*

Psalm 18:6

I clearly remember believing that I could do it all! I had just given birth to my second child, but I was sure that I could take care of my newborn and also maintain a wonderful relationship with my two-year-old, my spouse, my job, and my Lord. I believed that I was more than capable of meeting the challenge of mothering a newborn and a two-year-old simultaneously. I thought I was full of wisdom and strong enough to handle anything on my own. My husband offered to lend a hand and sometimes has fixed dinner. Even so, the late night and early morning demands from my toddler and my nursing infant have overwhelmed me. Finally, I cried out to the Lord.

APPLICATION

The Lord watches what we do. He sees how frustrated and weary we get, especially when things don't seem to work out as we planned. He's right there, waiting for us to recognize our need of Him. We work hard just to stay above water—but our "independence" ship seems to be sinking. As long as we are determined to handle life on our own, we will find ourselves in this struggle. But it's never too late to turn to the Lord; He will rescue us.

Identify your greatest point of frustration today. Then send out an S.O.S.: Seek Our Savior. When you call out to Him, He will answer. He is waiting on you.

PRAYER

Lord, I need to hear clearly from You today. I need peace. I need Your help! Please rescue me. In Jesus' name, I pray. Amen.

DAY 4 / FAITH, COMPLETE TRUST
POSITIVE DEPENDENCE...

"But without faith it is impossible to please him: for he that cometh to God must believe that he is, and that he is a rewarder of them that diligently seek him."

Hebrews 11:6

My mom raised five children. The Lord graced her by surrounding her with the support and wisdom of her mother and other relatives. She regularly gathered us together to pray, or she sought the Lord on our behalf—sometimes with urgent cries for help. But she trusted God to sustain her, recognizing that she was dependent on the Lord and Him alone.

APPLICATION

Christ loves to hear us say, "I can't do this without You." When we come to understand that our dependence is faith, and that faith is complete trust, we will begin to experience some invaluable encounters with Him. He waits for our uplifted hands. He is blessed when we cry out to Him. Come to Him, seek His presence, and trust in Him.

Look up several verses about faith. Then check a thesaurus for synonyms of faith. Who in the Bible showed faith? Consider how your life is different because of your faith, and praise God for it.

PRAYER

Lord, I want to please You. I know I am human and I am weak; this brings me into a positive position of dependency on You. Today I see. Today I hear. I depend on You, Lord. In Jesus' name, I pray. Amen.

DAY 5 / "I DO"

WITH JESUS AT THE ALTAR...

"For I know whom I have believed, and am persuaded that he is able to keep that which I have committed unto him against that day."
2 Timothy 1:12b

Scene 1

A man and a woman stand at their church's altar along with their pastor, who has just begun the wedding ceremony. It's time for the wedding vows; the pastor has asked the husband-to-be to state his vow.

Man to Woman: I promise to love and to cherish you, in sickness and in health, for better and for worse, until death do us part.

Pastor: Will you take this man to be your lawfully wedded husband?

Woman: I do.

Scene 2

God is present and ready to be in the woman's life. He will stand by His vow.

God to Woman: I promise to love and to cherish you. There will be no sickness I cannot heal; you will have divine health. You will always be better; you will never worsen. And with Me, you will experience eternal life; we'll never part.

Woman: I do, Lord. I D-O—I depend on God and obey the Word of God.

APPLICATION

What a great declaration and commitment, especially in Scene 2! The definition of the word do brings great revelation to the seeking spirit: To bring into existence; to finish; complete; an unopened end. No one can depend on God without obeying Him. Dependency in itself involves trust: He provides the direction, what He says is the truth, and what He promises is what He will do. Complete dependency requires that we trust and obey Him. When God makes a covenant—a promise to us—unlike our promises, He keeps His covenants. He is faithful from beginning to end. He is waiting for our commitment.

Picture yourself at the altar with the Lord, standing face-to-face. Hear Him declare His love for you and His faithfulness to you. Remember, He cannot lie. Now it's your turn. As you say, "I do," embrace the power of the words. Your commitment to depend on and obey God solidifies the relationship for eternity.

PRAYER

Lord, accept me today as Your dependent bride. I want to spend eternity with You. Yes, "I do." In Jesus' name. Amen.

SEPTEMBER

WEEK TWO: SINGLENESS

DAY 1 / SO MUCH LOVE

THERE'S POWER IN ONE...

"In this was manifested the love of God toward us, because that God sent his only begotten Son into the world, that we might live through him."

1 John 4:9

Harriet Tubman is a wonderful example of the power of one. A small woman with a debilitating injury, she "conducted" hundreds of slaves to the North to freedom in the days before the Civil War. Her single-handed accomplishments have been the subject of dozens of biographies, children's books, movies, TV shows, statues, museums, and holidays. Although sympathizers housed her and the people with her along the route known as the Underground Railroad, she was the one leading the way and returning again and again despite risks to her own health and liberty.

APPLICATION

The life of Harriet Tubman is a powerful image of what one person can do. But Jesus is a more powerful image. Harriet Tubman could not end the evil of slavery. Jesus ends our slavery to sin and death. Immeasurable power and strength comes from the Son of God.

What single effort can you undertake and complete that will demonstrate Christ's strength in you? Form a plan and carry it through to completion. As you implement your plan, pause and reaffirm your love for the Lord and your appreciation of what He does for you.

PRAYER

I really want to thank You, Lord! You love me so much that You sent Your only Son as ransom for me. No matter how busy I am with Your work, I want to take time to thank You. I am convinced there is strength in one, because You have proven it through Jesus. Amen.

APPRECIATE EVERY SINGLE SEASON...

"To every thing there is a season,
and a time to every purpose under the heaven."
Ecclesiastes 3:1

Lydia has been single all her life. She has a wonderful ministry. She works for a denominational newspaper, holds Bible study sessions in her home, frequently hosts international guests that come to learn about religious publishing, supports numerous missionaries, and frequently goes on short-term mission projects herself. Because she has never been encumbered by a family and has a steady job, she has had the income and freedom to visit and learn from deeply spiritual people of other places. She also has about 20 "godchildren" who call her Auntie Lydia, and she mentors a group of neighbor women. Her life is very full.

There have been times, however, when Lydia has acutely felt her singleness. She can feel very lonely, but she approaches these times by reminding herself that every life has the full range of seasons. The warmth of summer is followed by autumn's harvest. Winter can be a season of less activity. But spring always bursts forth next.

APPLICATION

Just as in this world we have the four seasons of winter, spring, summer, and fall—each with its own splendor and purpose—the Lord allows us to experience seasons in our lives. Though people have their favorite and least favorite seasons, there is a blessing in every period. God does not want you to dwell on an unwanted season. It will not last forever.

Sisters, use this season to gather a productive inventory. Consider how you have been "feeding" your body, mind, and spirit in healthy and unhealthy ways. What is healthy about your daily life? Now consider how unhealthy habits are diminishing your spiritual growth. Will your harvest this season be abundant or unsatisfying? Seek God's direction and purpose for how you can fill every single season.

PRAYER

Lord, I am a vessel with the heart to thrive during every season. If I am single, I am learning that You will help me learn how to occupy my time in productive, enriching ways that serve You. If I am married, I am learning that You will help me deepen my relationship with my husband. Help me learn to appreciate the value and purpose of every single season of my life. In Jesus' name. Amen.

DAY 3 / GOD'S SINGLE BLESSINGS

WHAT, YOU WANT ME TO BE A NUN?!

"He that is unmarried careth for the things that belong to the Lord, how he may please the Lord: But he that is married careth for the things that are of the world, how he may please his wife."

1 Corinthians 7:32b-33

At the water cooler, Shari gets in a discussion with Karen, a divorcée with two children; Mary, a single woman known for highly critical opinions of men; and Leola, a 65-year-old widow. Each woman expresses a different view of marriage.

Karen advises Shari to pray and seek God for the right mate. Because of Karen's experience with marriage, she stresses the importance of finding the right mate.

Mary says she has dated a lot and been engaged. But she thinks it's almost impossible to please a man, so she's given up the idea of ever finding a soul mate.

Then Leola tells the group that while everyone is entitled to their viewpoint, she challenges each woman to seek first to be close to the Lord. She urges them to strive right now, as single women, to use their singleness to draw close to God.

"Set the marriage issue aside," Leola says. "Focus instead on being a deeply spiritual single woman."

APPLICATION

Many of the devotions in this Bible deal with difficulties among women with families in finding time to be close to God. The single woman's life can be quite simple. In the early centuries of the church, communities of single people gathered together to do God's work, finding companionship in the community as a particularly efficient way to serve the Lord. Hospitals, schools, and libraries have been started and preserved by religious communities of single men and women.

Study 1 Corinthians 7. Write a list of the ways in which being single benefits you and allows you to be more dedicated to God. Make a list of the responsibilities that you do not have because you do not have a family. If you are married, reread the story above and consider how your perspective on marriage and motherhood can illuminate the decisions facing single women at your church.

PRAYER

God, help me to see the opportunities around me that are open to me primarily because I am single and do not have children. Help me to be grateful and to use my singleness to draw closer to You as I minister to others and gain the perspectives of married women around me. In the matchless name of Jesus. Amen.

DISCARD UNHEALTHY HABITS AND TIES...

"Then shall thy light break forth as the morning, and thine health shall spring forth speedily: and thy righteousness shall go before thee; the glory of the Lord shall be thy reward."

Isaiah 58:8

"What in the world are you doing, Patsy?" asked Norma. She sat at the patio table and ate the remaining French fries from her lunch.

"I'm exercising," Patsy replied. With enthusiasm, Patsy told Norma that she had begun a life maintenance program of exercise and diet that would help her to break unhealthy eating habits and acquire and maintain good health.

Norma, whose weight had yo-yoed as she tried various diets, said, "I would like to begin a training schedule myself, but I don't quite feel up to the challenge." Patsy knew why. Norma's heart was still being held hostage by old issues.

"Norma," Patsy said from her exercise mat, "You haven't put your past behind you. Allow the Lord to relieve you of your excess baggage. Let go of the unhealthy ties binding your soul. Let go!"

APPLICATION

Somehow, we think it is okay to overeat and not care about our bodies. When we take singlehood into account, this mindset says that we don't have a special person of the opposite sex to please with our body, so why bother eating healthily? God created our bodies and wants us to be healthy. God blesses us with the magnificence of His creation, so let's take care of this gift by making positive lifestyle changes.

If you have a tendency to eat poorly, do you know when and why? There are loads of books on healthy eating and exercise. Try out a few plans; but beforehand, get your doctor's approval for an eating and exercise plan that works the best for you. As you proceed with your changing lifestyle, ask Him to help you let go of your emotional baggage as well as your bad physical habits for a total healing experience.

PRAYER

Lord, as of this day, I commit my spirit, my body, and my mind to You. I must not allow "weight" of any kind to prevent me from selling out wholly to You, O Lord. Thank You for loving and caring about my body as well as my spirit. In Jesus' name. Amen.

DAY 5 / DECISIONS

WHERE TO FROM HERE?

"Thou wilt shew me the path of life: in thy presence is fulness of joy; at thy right hand there are pleasures for evermore."

Psalm 16:11

CEO Jim Jackson called a meeting with his staff one Monday morning. As the meeting began, he asked them to give him a written answer as to where they wanted to be in five years. At the close of the meeting, he took the papers, went to his office, and reviewed them. One response in particular stood out, from a relatively new hire named Ann.

Ann stated that her goal was to be the company's next CEO. Her plan was not to fast track, but to cross train in every area of the company. This would lead to worth, and worth to promotion, and one promotion would lead to another until she reached the top. Jim was impressed. Not only did she have a goal for her future, she had a plan and a way to execute it.

"This is the kind of person I like to promote," Jim said, smiling.

APPLICATION

Single people can be independent. With no one else to consider and with God's help, they can chart an unlimited course. This is the advantage of being single as it relates to the question: "Where to from here?" Our divine destiny—whether single or married—is to be content at His right hand, with pleasures that last forevermore.

Decide today that you will be the best you can be. Instead of waiting passively for someone to direct your future, ask yourself: Where to from here? Write down a briefly stated goal. Begin a plan with specific steps you can take from your present reality to the goal you have in mind. Check back on a regular basis to make sure you are still working your plan. Whatever your plan entails, decide that you will always go with God!

PRAYER

Lord, help me to understand what You are doing in my life. I will be content in You. I know that You will keep me because I want to be kept. I love You, Lord. Amen.

SEPTEMBER

WEEK THREE: PURITY

DAY 1 / LORD, GIVE ME A PURE HEART

THAT I MIGHT SERVE YOU...

*"For the grace of God that bringeth salvation hath appeared to all men,
Teaching us that, denying ungodliness and worldly lusts,
we should live soberly, righteously, and godly, in this present world;
Looking for that blessed hope, and the glorious appearing of the great
God and our Saviour Jesus Christ; Who gave himself for us,
that he might redeem us from all iniquity, and purify unto himself
a peculiar people, zealous of good works."*

Titus 2:11-14

Sally felt bad. Her company was downsizing and her best friend was fired. Sally knew that one of them probably would have to go. But she was happy to learn that she still had her job—because she really needed it. Now she wondered about the purity of her thoughts and feelings. Shouldn't she feel worse about her friend's predicament? She went to her pastor's wife for counsel.

APPLICATION

When Jesus Christ gave Himself for us, He knew that our thoughts and motives were not pure. Only through the grace of God and His salvation is it possible for us to repent of our selfishness and do good works. With the hand of Jesus guiding us, our life's work can truly be beautiful.

Examine recent thoughts, actions, and motives. Be completely honest with yourself. Confess any impurities to the Lord. Jesus came to redeem us from all our sins and to purify us so that we can live righteously in this world. Listen carefully to the voice of God about how you can go forward and fulfill His plan and purpose for your life. God equips everyone He calls. Read the prayer below to guide your next steps.

PRAYER

Lord, please give me a clean heart. Help me think like You. Cleanse me with hyssop, and I will be clean. Let me hear joy and gladness. Hide Your face from my sins, and blot out all my iniquity. Create in me a pure heart, O God, and renew a steadfast spirit within me. In Jesus' name. Amen.

DAY 2 / PURE HUMILITY

HUMBLE ME...

"Humble yourselves therefore under the mighty hand of God, that he may exalt you in due time."

1 Peter 5:6

Admitting the ugly truth about our past or our present will often cause us to humble ourselves and fall on our faces before God and beg for forgiveness. Then we can worship God with a pure heart.

After my husband and I started our first business and things were going great, I allowed myself to get caught up in its success. The business grew too fast. Then things started falling apart, and I realized that God had been left out of the picture. I thought I was in control, but God showed me that I was not. I needed to humble myself and admit the truth about my life.

APPLICATION

Humbly admitting to ourselves that we are wrong is the first step we need to take if we want to have a pure heart toward God. The next step is to confess it to God. This means that we swallow our pride and agree with God that we made a mistake. We can pray using David's words: "Search me, O God, and know my heart: try me, and know my thoughts: And see if there be any wicked way in me, and lead me in the way everlasting" (Psalm 139:23-24). Humility and confession before God also deepens our one-to-one relationship with the Father and imbues our spiritual walk with unique details.

27

With an appreciation for being in private with the Lord, ask Him to show you where you wronged someone. Ask God to forgive you and cleanse you—and then prayerfully consider going humbly to the person you wronged to apologize and ask forgiveness.

PRAYER

Lord, I am not perfect and I know it. Help me to understand this and repent. Restore me to Your grace so that I may live a pure life of service to You and speak words of life to others. Amen.

CHANGE YOUR THOUGHTS, CHANGE YOUR LIFE...

"Flee also youthful lusts: but follow righteousness, faith, charity, peace, with them that call on the Lord out of a pure heart."

2 Timothy 2:22

My life was not working out as I had hoped. I had done everything I could do, but some events were out of my control. I had to admit that my life was not meant to be under my control. Instead, God was in charge. I had to put my faith in Him, and not in myself, and call out to God for help in following His path.

APPLICATION

In this story, notice that we are not told many details. The turn of events in this person's life could involve a number of possibilities. That's because everyone faces these challenges and must learn that God calls us to live by pure faith—and to give up our need for control. If we are to leave behind our own plans for our lives, then we need to acknowledge the Scripture: "Let this mind be in you, which was also in Christ Jesus" (Philippians 2:5). This will push us out of our comfort zone and make faith possible.

In what areas of your life do you need to give up control? Write down the areas that are hardest to let go of. Then trust God to be with you as you press your way through your fear to faith.

PRAYER

God, I offer myself to You to build me so that I do Your will. Help me to turn my back on the bondage of self and follow You. Give me victory over my difficulties so that I may be a witness to Your power and Your love. Amen.

DAY 4 / PURE QUIETNESS

BE STILL AND KNOW THAT I AM GOD!

"Better is a handful with quietness, than both the hands full with travail and vexation of spirit."

Ecclesiastes 4:6

Larry did not know Jesus; but as he talked to me about his life, he told me that he needed to be away from everything and everyone to hear from God. I could not figure out why Larry had lived for the past two years by himself in an old, rundown home. A millionaire at one time, he somehow had lost everything. He claimed that this was only a temporary setback and that he would make a comeback. Meanwhile, he was being quiet, waiting for his time to come.

APPLICATION

In order to make the right choices in life, we have to get in touch with our souls. An awareness of your innermost being can strengthen your communication with God. Sometimes the only way to figure out what God is saying to us is to get really quiet. If you cringe at this idea, tell yourself also that to seek the Lord in quietness may be the wisest choice you could make. Remember that God is faithful. As you sit with Him, He will make Himself known to you.

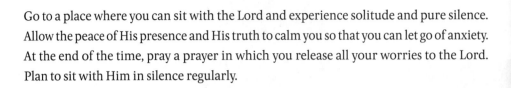

Go to a place where you can sit with the Lord and experience solitude and pure silence. Allow the peace of His presence and His truth to calm you so that you can let go of anxiety. At the end of the time, pray a prayer in which you release all your worries to the Lord. Plan to sit with Him in silence regularly.

PRAYER

Lord, with all purity, I ask You to teach me to be quiet so that I can hear a fresh word from You daily. I pray that in hearing Your still, small voice that I will not be anxious for anything. The beginning of true faith is the end of anxiety. Amen.

DAY 5 / PURITY IN PRAYER

PRAYER IS THE WOMB OF SUCCESS...

"Thus saith the Lord of hosts, Consider ye, and call for the mourning women.... And let them make haste, and take up a wailing for us, that our eyes may run down with tears, and our eyelids gush out with waters. Yet hear the word of the Lord, O ye women, and let your ear receive the word of his mouth, and teach your daughters wailing, and every one her neighbour lamentation."

Jeremiah 9a, 18, 20

As a woman of God, my foundation is prayer. I have learned through prayer that God is concerned with what is in my heart. When I was pregnant, God assured me that my children would be taught by Him. God has been faithful to keep His promise even when I am not faithful. God truly honors my prayers and those of my husband to guide and protect our children, bringing them closer to Him. I thank God for His well-conceived assurance.

APPLICATION

Prayer should be vital in the life of every home. As African American mothers, we need to see prayer as foundational to the Christian life and make it a priority. However, to truly pray effectively, we must first be women of the Word. A praying woman is an instrument of righteousness in our world. We should encourage one another to bring prayer into every area of life. We can pray in the car, at work, on the train, plane, bus, or subway. In addition, we need to do more than talk about prayer, for there is a power in prayer that few of us enter into. We can unleash this power mightily if we would "pray without ceasing."

Join or create a prayer circle. Ask a number of friends to pray with you once a week in person or over the phone. If you join with six of your friends, each person can be responsible to pray for the group one day. You might even have each member of the group fast on her day.

PRAYER

I will, with my whole heart, sing praises unto the most high God. I am no longer in bondage to sin. Thank You, Lord, for setting me free. In the righteous name of Jesus Christ, our Lord and Savior. Amen.

SEPTEMBER

WEEK FOUR: CELIBACY

DAY 1 / CELIBACY

TALK TO THE HAND!

*"Flee fornication.... What? know ye not that your body is the temple
of the Holy Ghost which is in you, which ye have of God,
and ye are not your own?"*

1 Corinthians 6:18a, 19

Heading home from singles ministry, Dorothy and her best friend Audrey shared opinions of the day's topic, celibacy. Audrey pursed her mouth in deep thought, pausing before she responded to Dorothy's insistence that Laurie, another member of the group, must have been lying when she said she was celibate.

Audrey softly replied, "Well, Dorothy, I'm celibate."

Dorothy was shocked. "Really? You don't look celibate!"

Audrey wondered what a celibate woman was supposed to look like. She felt completely normal and comfortable.

APPLICATION

Paul's letter to the Corinthians includes his views on celibacy (1 Corinthians 6:18; 7:34). Being celibate, a way to celebrate holiness in body and spirit, is defined as abstinence from sexual intercourse and is not a decision to be taken lightly. It is a promise that we make to God to honor His laws. We need to examine our close relationships and ask ourselves if they honor God.

Next time you are alone with someone you find attractive, ask yourself if God would be pleased with your thoughts and actions. Reflect on this question: Was your soul nourished by the experience? Perhaps you need to pray through Psalm 51.

PRAYER

Oh heavenly Lord, my Savior and my source of unequalled strength, I choose You to guide my actions. Help me to examine myself and determine how to fulfill my desires and needs appropriately. I know that only You, Lord, can fill every corner of my heart with everlasting joy. In the name of the Sovereign One, Christ Jesus. Amen.

SOMETIMES YOU JUST NEED TO PRAY!

"There hath no temptation taken you but such as is common to man: but God is faithful, who will not suffer you to be tempted above that ye are able; but will with the temptation also make a way to escape, that ye may be able to bear it."

1 Corinthians 10:13

Audrey decided this was what was known as "a teachable moment." She told her friend, "Dorothy, I have no idea how a celibate person is supposed to look, but I'm a normal woman. I made this decision with my body, mind, and soul. Celibacy is a choice I made many years ago; and sometimes I have to pray very hard, but I have never been more proud of any decision."

Dorothy nodded. "Well, you seem really convicted. But how do you remain celibate, Audrey? Aren't you dating?"

Audrey smiled. "Dorothy, make no mistake—deciding to be celibate is much easier than remaining celibate. But you've got to resist temptation."

APPLICATION

Celibacy is possible within or outside of a relationship. Both men and women can be celibate and still be happy and strongly connected to one another. But each person must agree that celibacy is best. Spending time together does not have to lead to sexual intercourse, and learning to enjoy a friend's company without sexual contact is possible. A smile, a glance, or a gentle touch goes a long way toward showing someone you care. The only part of the body required for trust, kindness, character, honesty, and love is the heart.

Consider the setting where you spend most of your time with the person you're becoming close to. Avoid being alone with a person you find sexually attractive because it can lead to intimacy. It can be difficult to plead for the Lord's help once you have started down the road of sexual arousal. Think about the situation before it gets out of control. The Bible encourages us to be content in our situation; whatever it is. Talk to God about your desires and ask Him to help you interpret them.

PRAYER

Oh precious Savior, You are sovereign, and You are great. As I think about my relationships, I know they have not always been pleasing in Your sight. Help me discover a relationship that allows me to grow as a Christian. Break the strongholds that keep me from blessing Your name, Father. In Jesus' name. Amen.

DAY 3 / SELF-CONTROL AND CELIBACY

WHAT'S GOOD TO YOU AIN'T ALWAYS GOOD FOR YOU!

"Can a man take fire in his bosom, and his clothes not be burned?"
Proverbs 6:27

Dorothy had more to talk about with her friend. "Audrey, sometimes I find that I have no self-control."

Audrey thought of a different way to describe her viewpoint. "Dorothy, if you put a pot of water on the heat long enough, it will start to boil. If you get too close to that pot, you could harm yourself."

"So, what are you trying to say?"

"Don't even put the pot on, Dorothy. You may feel the effects of the steam for a long time."

"Well, it doesn't hurt to slip up every now and then, right? You're not hurting anyone, right?"

"Dorothy, you hurt yourself when you don't exercise self-control. Your soul knows it as well as your body."

APPLICATION

What are the perils of a bad sexual relationship? Peter warns us, "Abstain from fleshly lusts, which war against the soul" (1 Peter 2:11b). When a bond is forged through intimacy, it is not easily broken. In our world of instant gratification, casual sex can lead to despair, loneliness, guilt, and low self-esteem. Only God can satisfy our hearts with a true and everlasting love, and only He knows what we want and need. Remember, "Your Father knoweth what things ye have need of, before ye ask him" (Matthew 6:8b).

Consider how soon you became intimate in the past. Now consider whether the intimacy was your decision. If the decision had been solely yours, would the timing have been the same? Why or why not? Read a few Christian books about sexual intimacy and re-examine your thoughts about intimacy and self-control. Above all, ask God for temperance, tolerance, and restraint as you let God be your guide.

PRAYER

Omnipotent God, You have been so faithful in Your dealings with me. I want to do Your will. Help me in my relationships. I have not always kept Your commandments, Lord, and I ask for forgiveness. Speak to me now, and let me hear what You say. Amen.

DAY 4 / SELF-ESTEEM AND CELIBACY

YOU ARE A ROYAL PRIESTESS WORTHY OF THE BEST!

"Who can find a virtuous woman? for her price is far above rubies.
She perceiveth that her merchandise is good: her candle goeth
not out by night."

Proverbs 31:10, 18

"Audrey, you may be right," Dorothy said to her friend. "Sometimes I got too close, too soon. But it is so hard to find someone who is real." Dorothy shook her head, briefly remembering relationships that ended on a bad note. "I get scared that if I am not in a relationship, my friends will think I am too choosy. I don't want to be seen as thinking I am better than others. After all, Audrey, I'm not all that."

"Oh, Dorothy, you are all that, and then some." Audrey turned toward her friend. "You are a royal priestess. You belong to God. You are God's beautiful creation. You deserve the best that God has to offer. Don't ever let anyone tell you differently, Dorothy."

APPLICATION

Too many times, we women of color act like Dorothy. Our color, size, hair texture, body shape, or socioeconomic status become reasons for feeling we are not worthy of God's blessings. So we seek comfort in superficial indulgences, including sexual indulgences.

41

Sometimes we forfeit our precious bodies to temptation and momentary pleasure, and celibacy gets disregarded.

The Bible tells us about many Black women. We can read about an African queen, the ruler of a vast kingdom (1 Kings 10:1-3). The Song of Solomon is a poem written in tribute to a Shulamite princess (1:5). Jesus sees our beauty, so we need to see ourselves as beautiful people. Your body is your esteemed possession, a living, breathing, sacred instrument; guard its purity and treat it with care. "But ye are a chosen generation, a royal priesthood, an holy nation, a peculiar people" (1 Peter 2:9a).

Look at yourself in the mirror and say, "I am worthy of all God has to give me. I am sometimes frail, weak, tired, angry, hurt, and sinful; but I am important. I will take control of my body and soul." Then admit and repent of your sins. Acknowledge that God loves you and treasures you. Each day appreciate your body, and treat it as a sacred, beautiful extension of your soul. Each week, write down one reason why your body is to be cherished.

PRAYER

Oh, God of my salvation, help me to value myself as a person. Help me to value my body as a sacred instrument, a temple of holiness and celibacy. I ask for Your Spirit to teach me. May Your will be done in my life. I am a new creature in You, Jesus. Amen.

DAY 5 / CELIBACY AND WHOLENESS

SAVING ALL OF MY LOVE FOR YOU, LORD...

"That he no longer should live the rest of his time in the flesh to the lusts of men, but to the will of God."

1 Peter 4:2

Dorothy said, "I truly understand what you are saying, Audrey. I guess I never really saw myself as God sees me. Celibacy is such a big decision, but now I know it's possible. It's achievable."

The two women hugged each other and had a few moments of prayer. Then Dorothy said, "Thanks so much."

Audrey smiled. "The road I've chosen isn't easy, Dorothy, but then again nothing worth having ever is, right? Just remember, I'm here for you and so is God."

APPLICATION

It is important to examine your beliefs about yourself. As a beautiful Black woman, you have a place and purpose on this earth. As a Christian, you have a destiny. Your focus should first and foremost be on the kingdom of heaven. Concentrate on being the best Christian you can be. You will fail at times, but you will also have triumphs. Celibacy can be one of your victories. Sacrificing physical desires is a way to honor God. It strengthens our faith.

Make a two-year plan for yourself and write it in a journal. At six-month intervals, catalog the positive changes you want to make. For each change, find a corresponding Scripture to encourage you on your journey. Make a step-by-step plan related to celibacy based on the readings of the last five days. Pray this Scripture when the going gets tough: "I can do all things through Christ which strengtheneth me" (Philippians 4:13).

PRAYER

My God, You are the great I AM. Cleanse my heart and my soul now, Jesus, so that there is nothing between us. I ask to be made whole. Place me on the path of righteousness for Your name's sake. Guide me by Your marvelous light. In the name of Jesus, I pray. Amen.

OCTOBER

WEEK ONE: GOODNESS

DAY 1 / THE POWER OF GOODNESS

TO WHOM DO YOU LISTEN?

"The goodness of God leadeth thee to repentance."
Romans 2:4b

Once upon a time, a very angry young woman regularly rode into the king's court and tore up everything in sight. One day, she was caught. The decree was to put her to death. But the king said, "No, let her determine her own fate."

The king explained, "On one side we will put people to encourage her, and on the other side we will put people who will discourage her. I will put a cup of water in her hand. If she walks between the two groups of people from one end of the room to the other without wasting water, she will live."

The people on one side told her, "Come on, you can make it. You can do this."

On the other side the people told her, "You can't make it. You will die."

She made it across the room without spilling any water. The king asked her what side she listened to. She said, "Neither; I just concentrated on the cup."

If you listen to others' voices—either good or bad—you will be distracted. You have to focus on your goal.

APPLICATION

If we want to be good people in God's eyes, then we must focus on the goal of goodness and not worry about how other people see us. What is good in the world's eyes is not necessarily good in God's eyes. God is the ultimate judge, so we must train our eyes on Him to determine whether our behavior or attitude is good or bad. In this way, we can apply one of the fruits of the Holy Spirit to our lives.

Look in the mirror and tell yourself, "God loves me and is shaping me in His image." Say this three times a day for a week and feel the power of goodness.

PRAYER

Father, in Jesus' name, help me to be all I can be so that Your fruit of goodness may abound in me. I want Your people to see Your glory in me and then glorify You. Amen.

DAY 2 / OH, MY GOODNESS

MATURE WOMANHOOD...

*"We have a little sister, and she hath no breasts: what shall we do
for our sister in the day when she shall be spoken for?
If she be a wall, we will build upon her a palace of silver:
and if she be a door, we will inclose her with boards of cedar."*

Song of Solomon 8:8-9

Ciara entered her first foster home when she was nine years old, having been sexually abused by family members and hating everything and everybody. All she needed was to be loved and encouraged. Her foster mom recognized her pain and began to minister the Word of God to her concerning healing. After many years of prayer, patience, kindness, and love by her foster mom, teachers, and her pastor, Ciara went on to college. After she graduated and worked as counselor, Ciara opened a center for abused women.

APPLICATION

The passage from Song of Solomon speaks of an immature girl (one who has not yet developed breasts). She may become a wall, which describes someone who is impervious to sexual temptation—a woman who stands firm. Such a woman deserves praise. Or, she may become like a door—a woman who allows men to enter easily. If so, the writer says that we must built walls of cedar around her. Cedar is a wood that builders often use for boats and roofs because of its protective durability. Our boards of cedar will be the Word of God to protect our sister from immorality.

Think about the people in your life with whom you were close when you were approaching puberty. Did they encourage you to be a wall or a door? Write down the names of people from this time in your past and describe how they helped or hurt your process of maturing into womanhood.

PRAYER

Father, in Jesus' name, help me to be more aware of the conditions of my sisters around me. Help me know that if not for Your grace, I could be in their shoes. Let my treatment of all women I encounter serve as a demonstration of Your lovingkindness. Amen.

DAY 3 / GOOD AND PLENTY

GOODNESS AND MERCY...

"Surely goodness and mercy shall follow me all the days of my life:
and I will dwell in the house of the Lord for ever."

Psalm 23:6

Mary Stone was newly divorced with four small children. The bills were due, no child support check had come in, and she had no financial support of any kind. Her first thought was to kill herself. If she did, the children would have the insurance money to live on. But who would raise the children? Mary began to focus on what she had. She was healthy. Her children were, too. They had food, and most importantly they had each other.

Gradually, the good days began to outweigh the bad ones. Even the bad ones could be used as stepping-stones to a higher quality of life. In the end, Mary Stone educated four children and got her doctorate in communications.

APPLICATION

Ever thought you could not make it or that you were too weak to fight for life? But if you were not strong you would not be here. Many slaves that were taken from the coast of Africa were killed on the way across the ocean, dying of the deplorable conditions of the Middle Passage, or they took their own lives. But your ancestors were among those who made it. If they had not been strong enough to make it, you would not be here.

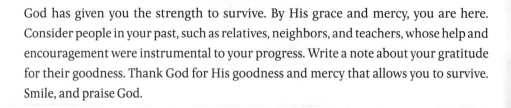

God has given you the strength to survive. By His grace and mercy, you are here. Consider people in your past, such as relatives, neighbors, and teachers, whose help and encouragement were instrumental to your progress. Write a note about your gratitude for their goodness. Thank God for His goodness and mercy that allows you to survive. Smile, and praise God.

PRAYER

Father, in Jesus' name, Your Word says to let the weak say, "I am strong" and the poor say, "I am rich." I say I am strong and rich in Your goodness. Amen.

DAY 4 / STRANGE FRUIT
GRAFTED ON TO THE VINE...

"I am the true vine, and my Father is the husbandman."
John 15:1

Gerri knew there was something missing in her life. She felt a void in her life but didn't know why. One day, she asked a coworker, "Why are you happy all the time?" She couldn't figure out why nothing ever seemed to bother the woman.

Gerri's coworker shared her faith in Christ with Gerri, and Gerri's life was changed that day. She got saved and filled with the Holy Spirit. Gerri was the fruit of her coworker's faith.

APPLICATION

Over the past two days, we have talked about goodness, one of the fruits of the Spirit. It has been said that "the fruit doesn't fall far from the tree"—in other words, the type of fruit is determined by the type of tree. When you are connected to Jesus, the true vine, you will produce good fruit. Jesus said, "I am the vine, ye are the branches: He who abideth in me, and I in him, the same bringeth forth much fruit: for without me ye can do nothing" (John 15:5).

What would you consider to be the fruit of your relationship to Christ? How does Christ's life in you help you to produce good fruit instead of bad? Make a list of the good fruit that you can produce.

PRAYER

Father, I come to You in the name of Jesus. Graft me onto Your vine. Help me to produce fruit that is pleasing to You. Let my fruit be good, as is all fruit that comes from the vine of Jesus. Amen.

DAY 5 / GOODY TWO-SHOES

BEHOLD, A GOOD, GODLY WOMAN...

"And God saw every thing that he had made, and, behold, it was very good. And the evening and the morning were the sixth day."

Genesis 1:31

India had earned the label "goody two-shoes" because she refused to listen to gossiping coworkers. She did not go with the crowd for drinks after work, and she left parties when they included men with an agenda other than what God would honor. She knew who she was in the Lord, and she knew it was perfectly normal to be a lady of character—respectful, good, godly, and blessed.

APPLICATION

"Goody two-shoes" can have a negative or a positive meaning. It refers to someone of high moral character. But it can also refer to someone who is so proud and stuck-up that everyone around her looks bad. Fortunately for all of us, we are not judged by what we do but what we believe. We don't have to be a goody two-shoes in order to inherit eternal life. We don't have to be perfect or think we are! We just have to believe.

Who do you know that is considered a "goody two-shoes"? Why is she or he labeled that way? Is the label being used positively or negatively?

PRAYER

Father, thank You that I do not need to be perfect. Thank You that I can make mistakes. Help me to make fewer and fewer mistakes as I grow in You. In Jesus' name, teach me how to show high moral character so that I can honor You in all that I do. Amen.

OCTOBER

WEEK TWO: JOY

DAY 1 / GOD'S GREAT JOY

HE'S GOT THAT JOY...

"But the fruit of the Spirit is love, joy, peace, longsuffering, gentleness, goodness, faith, meekness, temperance: against such there is no law."
Galatians 5:22-23

Every weekday evening, Joyce picked up her three-year-old daughter from her babysitter's house. Next door, an old man sat on the porch in his wheelchair. Each day, he said to Joyce, "Ain't our God a good God?"

Each day, Joyce answered, "Yes, sir. He sure is." Joyce asked her babysitter about the old man. She told Joyce that he lost his wife to cancer two years before. Soon after that, he was stricken with diabetes, lost his sight almost completely, and was confined to a wheelchair. A nurse came by every day to help him.

"Wow," said Joyce. "You would never know he's been through any of that."

Her babysitter agreed. "I said the same thing when he told me his story, and all he said to me was, 'Ain't our God a good God?'"

APPLICATION

The Bible tells us in Galatians 5:22 that joy is a fruit of the Holy Spirit. If you have the Holy Spirit dwelling within, joy is one of the works that His presence will accomplish. Joy is not the absence of trouble; it is the absence of depression during trouble. When you have the joy of the Lord within, you'll find yourself encouraging others even when your own problems haven't been solved. When the Holy Spirit produces joy in you, He is actually covering you with a part of His divine nature that won't allow the trials of life to stick to you.

Take a moment and reflect on the true meaning of joy. Then write a list of all the things that make you happy. Ask yourself if there is anything on your list that Jesus can't give you. Then ask yourself if there is anything on your list that can give you joy. If you answered no to both questions, begin today to allow Jesus to impart His joy into your inner being.

PRAYER

God, I thank You for being so loving that You sent the Holy Spirit to dwell within me and give me Your joy. Thank You, God, for the joy of the Lord, which is truly our strength! In Jesus' name, I pray. Amen.

DAY 2 / THE LOOK OF JOY

YOU'VE GOT THAT LOOK!

"To appoint unto them that mourn in Zion, to give unto them beauty for ashes, the oil of joy for mourning, the garment of praise for the spirit of heaviness; that they might be called trees of righteousness, the planting of the Lord, that he might be glorified."

Isaiah 61:3

Deneen calls her cousin Sasha a "people magnet." Everywhere Sasha goes people are drawn to her. Just the other day Sasha was renewing her driver's license. When she got to the window, the lady at the counter told her she had an outstanding parking ticket that needed to be paid first.

In order to pay the ticket, Sasha would have to step out of line. Before Sasha could turn to move, the lady at the counter said, "I'm gonna be nice today. Just write out your check, and I'll walk it over to the cashier so you won't lose your place in line. I don't know why I'm doing this for you, but there's something about your face. I can just tell that you're a nice person who would probably do the same thing for me."

Sasha thanked the lady for being so kind, but added, "Ma'am, it's not me. It's the joy of the Lord working inside me."

APPLICATION

The joy of the Lord inside you produces an outward glow. The look of joy is attractive. People want to be around those who have the joy of the Lord. Joy works similarly to laughter but on a deeper level because joy is a characteristic of God Himself. Isaiah 61:3 says that the Lord will give the oil of joy. God wants to saturate us with the oil of His joy until we are drenched, soaked, immersed, flooded, permeated, and dripping with it so that it will rub off on someone else.

Today, take a good, honest look at yourself. Do you carry with you the look of joy? Are you able to lighten the atmosphere of a room just by walking into it? If you have the look of joy, then seek the Lord's guidance to help you maintain it. If not, pray for a good dose of joy.

PRAYER

Dear Lord, I love You and acknowledge You as the Light of the World. Today I ask that You saturate me with the oil of Your joy. Please impart in me the glow and radiance that comes from having Your joy. Thank You, Lord. In Jesus' name, I pray. Amen.

DAY 3 / COUNT IT ALL JOY

WHERE'S THE JOY IN THIS?

"Count it all joy when ye fall into divers temptations; Knowing this, that the trying of your faith worketh patience. But let patience have her perfect work, that ye may be perfect and entire, wanting nothing."

James 1:2-4

Sarah adopted John when he was three weeks old. John was born severely disabled and was abandoned by his natural mother. Several doctors told Sarah that John would require care for the rest of his life. After taking care of John for seven years, Sarah realized that the doctors were correct.

One day, Sarah's neighbor stopped by to return a borrowed vacuum cleaner. As she was leaving, she said, "Sarah, you have to know that John's situation is hopeless. No one would blame you if you sent him to a residential facility."

Sarah looked at her and said, "Thirty-seven years ago, someone found me in a garbage can with my umbilical cord still connected. I lived in a group home for eight years, and I was so afraid to speak that every doctor labeled me retarded. When I turned nine, a woman adopted me. My new mom realized that I wasn't retarded, just love-starved. She loved me into the woman you see today. I know that John will never walk or talk, and I know that he knows he's loved. There's no greater joy than that."

APPLICATION

How can we count temptations and trials as joy? Read James 1:2-4 in the New Living Translation. We should count our troubles as opportunities for joy because of the endurance and patience that will be produced in us. When the Bible says we ought to count it all joy, the word count means to consider or to think. So we are to consider or think of what's going to be produced in our lives as a result of this present trial or trouble.

Jesus is our perfect example (see Hebrews 12:2). Knowing what His sufferings would produce enabled Jesus to look to the joy that would come later. After our faith is tested, then endurance will grow. As a result, we will be ready for anything.

Think about a trial that you may be facing right now. Think back a few years ago and ask yourself: If I had to face this trial back then, would I have been able to handle it by counting it as joy? If you're not sure, watch how God will develop you as you face and overcome each new trial.

PRAYER

Dear heavenly Father, I thank You for every trial that You allow to come my way because You have a perfect plan for me. Today I ask that You grant me the ability to count every hardship and every disappointment as an opportunity for joy. In Jesus' name, I pray. Amen.

DAY 4 / THE FULLNESS OF JOY

CAN I GET ANOTHER REFILL, PLEASE?

"Thou wilt shew me the path of life: in thy presence is fulness of joy; at thy right hand there are pleasures for evermore."

Psalm 16:11

One day Charise, in college about 300 miles from home, got homesick and called her mom. But her mom's answering machine picked up, and Charise hung up without leaving a message. Her mom called later; and after they exchanged a few words, she said Charise sounded like something wasn't right. Charise told her mom she just wanted to hear her voice. Her mom understood that she was homesick, and they stayed on the phone well past midnight.

Later that week, someone at the front desk buzzed Charise, telling her to come down and pick up her flowers! Thinking that her mom must have sent the bouquet, Charise ran to the pay phone in her hallway and called her mom. The answering machine picked up, and this time Charise left a message: "Mom, thank you so much for the flowers. I still miss you, though. Love you." Before Charise could hang up, she heard her mother say, "I love you, too, baby." Her mom was standing behind her in the hallway!

APPLICATION

The Bible tells us in Psalm 16:11 that in God's presence there is fullness of joy. That's where the reservoir is—in the presence of God our Father. So you've got to get into His presence. You may not have much desire to go to church or get on your knees and pray. But praise be to God, His presence can meet you right where you are (see Psalm 139). He is waiting to fill you once again with His wonderful joy.

Take this mini-quiz to see if you need a refill of God's joy: 1) Have you been feeling depressed for long periods of time with or without good reason? 2) Have you lost an interest in reading or hearing the Word of God? 3) Are you easily upset by people or situations that wouldn't normally bother you? If you answered yes to any of these questions, cry out to the Lord; He is listening and will provide for you.

PRAYER

Sweet Jesus, I am thankful that Your presence can reach me. Lord, I need a refill of your joy. I know that once I feel Your presence, I'll receive Your joy. So, please Lord, fill me with Your joy until it overflows. In Jesus' name, I pray. Amen.

DAY 5 / KINGDOM PEOPLE CRAVE JOY

GOT JOY?

"For the kingdom of God is not meat and drink; but righteousness, and peace, and joy in the Holy Ghost."

Romans 14:17

Mrs. Peterson was one of the most frugal shoppers in town. She practically lived at the dollar store. If you looked in her cupboard, you would only see generic products. Mrs. Peterson liked things cheap, and she wasn't ashamed of being thrifty. She believed that if there was a cheaper price for something, why pay more?

Most folks didn't know that Mrs. Peterson was very wealthy. Her late husband had left her a rich estate. One of her friends once asked her why she was so miserly. Mrs. Peterson said, "I don't put value on stuff. By the end of May, I will have put 12 kids from our church through college. Last week, I sent five of our church's missionaries to Johannesburg, South Africa, and they have enough funding to stay there for a year so that they can really do some good. That's what I spend my money on—things that last."

APPLICATION

We, as Christians, so often put our focus and attention on the things of this world and whatever pertains to the kingdom of God takes a back seat. This week's focus has been on joy, but has joy been your focus? If the things of God are not a big deal to us, then our

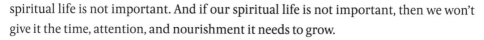

spiritual life is not important. And if our spiritual life is not important, then we won't give it the time, attention, and nourishment it needs to grow.

On a scale of 1 to 10 (10 being the most important), rate the following priorities: 1) Expressing daily the fruit of the Spirit. 2) Making a good impression on the people at my job or at church. 3) Pleasing God and spending time learning about the things of God. 4) Obtaining financial wealth and security for my family and me. Think about adjusting the importance of your priorities. Begin today to give the things of God first priority and watch your spiritual life flourish and grow.

PRAYER

Dear heavenly Father, I ask that You kindle the fire of my desire for the things that come from heaven above. I want the things of God. I want to experience Your joy in its fullness. These things I ask in the precious and matchless name of Jesus Christ. Amen.

OCTOBER

WEEK THREE: KINDNESS

DAY 1 / LOVINGKINDNESS

THE NATURE OF GOD...

"But after that the kindness and love of God our Saviour toward man appeared, Not by works of righteousness which we have done, but according to his mercy he saved us.

Titus 3:4-5a

Nikisha visited Mrs. Lola twice a week at Maranatha Residential Home. Mrs. Lola was usually alone because she had a temper the other residents could not bear.

"Hi, Mrs. Lola," said Nikisha.

Mrs. Lola squirmed. "I wish you would go away. I don't know why you even bother coming here. Everyone says I'm a grouchy old woman."

"I bother because I care about you, Mrs. Lola," Nikisha replied. Grouchy old women need kindness, too. Besides, I enjoy being around you. I have learned so much by visiting you."

"Like what?" the old lady murmured.

"I've learned how to look beyond people's faults, actions, and behaviors. I've learned to be kind to others no matter what. You see, God shows us lovingkindness in the midst of all of our faults, and we are to follow His example. We must love when love isn't given. We must be kind when kindness isn't there. I've learned to do that."

A tiny smile appeared in Mrs. Lola's eyes. The elderly woman was not as lonely as before.

APPLICATION

Lovingkindness is an attribute of God's character. Lovingkindness may also be translated as "loyal love." God's anger is for a moment but His loyal love is forever a part of His mercy, and His mercy accepts and blesses us when we deserve to be totally rejected. God wants us to have that same attribute. He wants us to be kind to others as a part of our heavenly growth. That way we learn to fulfill our destiny.

Identify the situations in your life that call for you to show lovingkindness. Even though you may have done so already, try this week to show lovingkindness in ways that you have not done before.

PRAYER

Father God, help me yield to Your Spirit inside. Help me use every situation in my life as a way to grow. Teach me how to show lovingkindness to all that I come in contact with. In Jesus' name. Amen.

DAY 2 / KINDNESS, THE YOU INSIDE

LET A KIND GOD MAKE A KIND YOU...

"Give to him that asketh thee, and from him that would borrow of thee turn not thou away."

Matthew 5:42

"You've been unusually quiet," his mother remarked as she gave Jason the salt. "Is something bothering you?"

"Anthony is mad at me because I wouldn't let him borrow my basketball," Jason blurted.

"That's not like you, Jason. Anthony is your best friend. What's the big deal about letting him borrow your basketball?" his sister Carmen asked.

"The big deal is that it's my ball, and I don't have to let him use it if I don't want to."

"Jason, it's wrong not to let people your borrow things at times," his mother explained. "You have to be kind and generous to others if you plan on keeping them as your friends. Let Anthony know that it's okay to borrow from you as long as he takes care of your things and returns them."

"I guess," said Jason. "I know I used to let him use my stuff. I don't know what happened lately."

"It's not always easy to hear the truth, is it?" his mother asked.

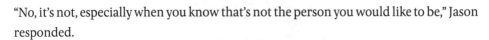

"No, it's not, especially when you know that's not the person you would like to be," Jason responded.

"It's always hard to face the real you, but God can help you make that change."

APPLICATION

Has someone close to you told you about an element of your attitude or behavior that opposes the fruit of the Spirit? Have you seen a part of yourself lately that you think God would like to change? Pray to Him about a character trait that needs changing and ask Him to work on it with you.

PRAYER

Father, I am opening my heart and allowing You to prune me so that I can become the Christian You want me to be. Help me to listen and look to the Spirit for guidance. In Jesus' name. Amen.

KINDNESS OF THE HEART...

"Now there was at Joppa a certain disciple named Tabitha, which by interpretation is called Dorcas: this woman was full of good works and almsdeeds which she did."

Acts 9:36

"What are you baking, Madea?" Little Angie asked her neighbor.

"I'm baking cookies for the homeless people at Mercy House," answered Madea.

"How come you do so many things like that for other people?" Angie asked.

"I enjoy making things, and giving them away." Madea smiled. "When you make things at school or at church, you give them to your mama and me, don't you?"

Angie nodded. "I do, but you are kind to people you don't even know."

"Angie," Madea said, "I like being like Dorcas in the book of Acts. She was always doing kind things for others and helping the poor."

Angie asked, "When you do kind things for others, how does that make you feel?"

Madea smiled. "It makes my heart glad to see them enjoy something I gave. And I'm not looking for anything in return."

"When I get older, I'm going to do things for other people, too—like you and Dorcas," Angie decided.

"You don't have to wait that long," Madea said. "Give me a hand with these cookies, and we'll deliver them together."

APPLICATION

Like Dorcas, Madea, and Angie, each of us has opportunities to do kind things for others. God tells us in 2 Peter 1:7 to add human kindness to our godliness and charity to our human kindness. As Christians, we have a responsibility to walk freely in kindness even if no one notices. God wants us to bear kind fruit and make a difference in someone's life. This nourishes love for the recipient and the giver, and increases our willingness to overlook each other's weaknesses.

Bake something and give it to a homeless shelter in your city. Or take someone who doesn't have a car to the grocery store. Or think of some other act of kindness and do it today. Notice the effect on you of the gratitude you receive.

PRAYER

Lord, let me stretch a helping hand to those in need, not just to the people I know but to those whom I don't know. Let my heart be kind; let me always want to do Your perfect will. In Jesus' name. Amen.

DAY 4 / KINDNESS TO FAMILY
TEACHING KINDNESS BY EXAMPLE...

"Let no man despise thy youth; but be thou an example of the believers, in word, in conversation, in charity, in spirit, in faith, in purity."
1 Timothy 4:12

The aroma of Grandpa's Sunday morning breakfast wafted through the house: buttermilk pancakes, bacon, scrambled eggs, and freshly squeezed orange juice.

"Rise and shine," Grandpa shouted. "Breakfast is ready." This was Grandpa's routine and had been for many years.

Six-year-old Kyle quickly washed his face and hands, and ran into the kitchen. Grandpa was sitting at the table with a huge smile on his face. He enjoyed watching his grandson enjoy breakfast. Kyle ate his food while watching his grandpa. When he was done, he dropped the messy plate, fork, and cup into the sink.

"I want to wash them today, Grandpa," he insisted.

Grandpa thought for a moment. "Okay," he said.

Kyle said, "I want to do something kind for my grandpa, who's always doing nice things for me."

APPLICATION

Our family members will learn from our daily actions and our words. Therefore, we must pay careful attention that our lives at home are in line with the Word of God. In addition, children behave as they see adults around them behaving; we pass on our kind words and deeds to them as we shape their attitudes and actions, and the fruit of the Spirit lives on through them.

Pay attention to how you are presenting yourself in front of your family. Teach them kindness by the example you lead. Do something especially nice for family members on the spur of the moment. Don't announce it in advance, and don't expect anything in return.

PRAYER

Father, in the name of Jesus, I commit myself to walk in the Word. I recognize that Your Word is integrity, and I trust my life to its provisions. Help me be kind to family members. Amen.

DAY 5 / KINDNESS BY ALL MEANS

BEING KIND UNDER EVERY CIRCUMSTANCE...

"Put on therefore, as the elect of God, holy and beloved, bowels of mercies, kindness, humbleness of mind, meekness, longsuffering."
Colossians 3:12

Sarah moved quickly through the store. In the produce section, she picked out collard greens, onions, green peppers, and celery. "How I dread this time of year," she murmured while moving past several people who were jammed together near the candy aisle.

Even though Halloween was almost two weeks away, it seemed that a lot of people decided to purchase the bags of candy that typically were bought around this time. To Sarah's mind, it was too soon; and the way people were acting—as though they were last-minute shoppers on Christmas Eve—she just wanted to gather her items and go home.

Sarah headed for the checkout line. Suddenly a middle-aged woman, coming out of nowhere with a loaded cart, bumped Sarah's cart and knocked her produce to the floor. The woman immediately became irate, blaming Sarah for the collision.

With a deep breath, Sarah reminded herself that not everyone is kind, patient, or considerate. Suddenly she remembered something: Jesus always is kind. She backed her cart up so the woman could go in front of her. Then she stooped down and retrieved her groceries.

APPLICATION

Being kind under every circumstance is something we are to strive for daily. We must refuse the evil and choose the good. Our flesh may want to get irate with others, but if we want to rule over the enemy we must say: "It is no longer I who live, but Christ who lives in me" (see Galatians 2:20).

Determine to be kind even when the circumstances around you are not. Memorize a verse such as Galatians 2:20 to encourage Christ's kindness to embed itself within you. Repeat the verse frequently throughout the day so you are thoroughly familiar with its meaning and can access it as the need arises. Ask the Holy Spirit to get involved in everything you do today.

PRAYER

Father, help me to be kind. Help me live a life directed by You so that the enemy cannot rule over me. Clothe me with compassion, love, and kindness. In Jesus' name. Amen.

OCTOBER

WEEK FOUR: PEACE

DAY 1 / PEACE OF MIND

LORD, JUST GIVE ME SOME PEACE!

"Thou wilt keep him in perfect peace, whose mind is stayed on thee: because he trusteth in thee."

Isaiah 26:3

Denise told her friend Terri, "My doctor said I have an ulcer because I've been worrying too much. I don't know what to do, Terri."

"Have you tried giving it to Jesus? Take your burdens to the altar and leave them."

A little irritated, Denise said, "I've done that!" She told Terri. "My burdens are stubborn."

Denise's friend laughed and said, "Well, they do have that tendency. But giving your burdens to Jesus is a continual process. God wants you to have peace of mind."

APPLICATION

Deep contentment involves wholly trusting in God and keeping your mind constantly on Him. In every decision, action, and reaction, you should consider the will of Christ and His divine purpose for your life. Then, put your trust in Him fully—therein you will find perfect peace and be able to apply this fruit of the Holy Spirit to your life. Walking in peace is an ongoing process, and it requires faith. If you study your Bible daily, you are transformed by the renewing of your mind (Romans 12:2).

When a troubling issue comes to mind, visualize yourself writing a note: "To Jesus: I give You ____. You are now the executor of this problem estate." Picture yourself taking the note to a locked container with a slot for Jesus marked, Cast All Your Cares on Him and pushing the note through the slot.

PRAYER

Lord, Your Word says that I should be transformed by the renewing of my mind. I welcome You to occupy my thoughts. Take complete residence there so that I might apply peace to my life. In the name of Jesus, I pray. Amen.

DO I ALWAYS HAVE TO BE THE PEACEMAKER?

"With all lowliness and meekness, with longsuffering, forbearing one another in love; Endeavoring to keep the unity of the Spirit in the bond of peace."

Ephesians 4:2-3

After church, Stephanie told the pastor's wife that she had been to see a doctor recently for sinus headaches. Another sister overheard the conversation and commented, "Are you still going to those doctors?" Stephanie, mildly shocked, smiled at the sister and did not respond.

After Stephanie ended her conversation with the pastor's wife and headed toward her car, she began talking to Jesus. She told Him that she was hurt by what the sister said about "going to those doctors." Then Stephanie began to think of how she could have responded. Her hand went to her hip as she told the sister off in her mind. But then the Holy Spirit whispered to her; she gave the anger to Jesus and let peace flow inside her. Humming to herself, she got in her car and headed home.

APPLICATION

The apostle Paul described a peacemaker as someone who possesses lowliness and meekness, longsuffering, and forbearance (Ephesians 4:2-3). A peacemaker must have a meek and lowly spirit and at times be longsuffering, accommodating, selfless, and resigned. Then there is forbearance, which involves lovingly exhibiting patience, self-control, restraint, tolerance, leniency, and mercy. Peacemaking is another fruit of the Spirit.

The next time someone tries your patience, smile! Most likely, you are responding to devilment. If you find the need to speak your peace, try this: Walk away from the situation and ask God to infiltrate your spirit. Ask Him to speak through you. Ask Him to direct what you should say or do. Then, find the appointed time to approach the brother or sister who jeopardized your contentment. Be patient, self-controlled, and merciful. Make peace!

PRAYER

Lord, help me to combat my inclination to get riled up and snap at my brother or sister. I know that I am wrestling against powers and principalities. As I endeavor to be called Your child, I pray the peacemaking spirit that You desire will abide in me and rule. In the name of Jesus, I pray. Amen.

DAY 3 / PEACE IN SPIRITUAL DELIBERATIONS
THE WISE WIN SOULS!

"And your feet shod with the preparation of the gospel of peace."
Ephesians 6:15

Patricia walked into the lunchroom at her job. She was happy to see her coworkers gathered at a table because she wanted to invite them to a revival at her church. The women had told her before that they belonged to other churches. But in Patricia's opinion, the women needed to change and she was not going to allow the devil to stop her from witnessing.

She walked over and said, "Praise the Lord, ladies."

"Hey," one dryly responded.

"Here's a flyer for a revival at my church." Patricia held out an announcement. "It's not too late to get your houses in order."

"My house is in order," Rebecca said.

Patricia said, "Not like the Bible says. You're going to be left when Jesus returns."

Rebecca stood up with her hands on her hips.

Diane said, "Sit down, Rebecca. Patricia, you make it seem like the only path to righteousness is at your church. If you stop judging others, someone might listen to you."

Rebecca pulled out a chair. "Have lunch with us."

Slowly, Patricia sat down. Maybe if she lightened up a bit, her coworkers would join her at the revival. She pulled her lunch from her bag as Diane asked about her church.

APPLICATION

Remember the religious leaders who sought to stone the adulterous woman? (See John 8:3-11.) They sought to be the final judge of her life. But only Jesus has that authority. Jesus told the religious leaders, "If you don't have any sin within you, throw a stone at her." They couldn't, because all people have sinned. If you consider your many imperfections, your spiritual deliberations will be peaceful instead of judgmental.

The next time you are witnessing or inviting someone to your church, do so with an attitude of love and peace. Inform people that God is real and He is all they will ever need. Share the Good News in a peaceful manner. Speak the truth in love.

PRAYER

Lord, help me to witness to Your children with peace on my lips. Stop all of my fleshly penchants to argue and give me Your Spirit of peace. Remind me that we are all sinners saved by grace. In Your name, I pray. Amen.

FOSTERING PEACE WITH LOVED ONES...

"And into whatsoever house ye enter, first say, Peace be to this house."
Luke 10:5

Zora angrily swung open the door to let her friend Clarenda enter.

"What's wrong with you?" Clarenda asked cautiously.

"Why did you come over?" Zora retorted.

"You were going to take me shopping with you this evening, remember? Maybe you'll feel better if you talk about what's upsetting you," Clarenda urged.

"No, you're just being nosy because you want to know my business," Zora declared.

Looking hurt, Clarenda headed back down the sidewalk. Zora watched her, wondering what she should do or say next.

APPLICATION

It is important that you try not to allow your trials to hinder or affect otherwise peaceful relationships. Unexpected and unwanted intrusions are bad enough. But it is worse when you invite additional turmoil. Imagine how differently the Crucifixion would have unfolded if Jesus berated His accusers. Instead, Jesus asked His Father to forgive

His executioners. Peace is stronger than chaos. If you are persistent, peace will prevail.

Start your day today by asking the Lord to allow peace to abide in you. If you have already started having a bad day, take a deep breath and ask God to help you implement peace.

PRAYER

Lord, assist me in thinking of creative ways to convert negative energy into peaceful energy. In the name of Jesus, I pray. Amen.

HOW CAN I HAVE PEACE WHEN THE DEVIL IS BUSY?

"These things have I spoken unto you, that in me ye might have peace.
In the world ye shall have tribulation: but be of good cheer;
I have overcome the world."

John 16:33

As Peggy began her morning prayers, the phone rang.

"Is this Peggy Withers?" the caller asked.

"Yes," she replied.

The caller asked, "Do you have a son at the university in Beaumont, Texas?"

Peggy responded, "Yes, who is this?"

The caller identified himself as a member of the Beaumont Police Department. They had brought her son in for questioning because of alleged involvement in a disturbance at a fraternity house. By law they had to release him to a parent or guardian.

"I'll catch the next flight out," Peggy assured the officer.

But when she notified her supervisor, he said her monthly reports were due; her pleadings went unheeded. Peggy began to cry out to the Lord, praying that He would **make a way.**

Once at the office, a coworker agreed to help her. As they worked feverishly, Peggy admitted why she needed to finish quickly. The coworker reassured her that everything would be all right.

A while later, Peggy's mail was delivered to her desk. Included was a letter from her favorite airline's frequent flyer program entitling her to a round-trip airline ticket.

Peggy was amazed. She called and got a reservation for that evening. Her coworker said, "See? Peace is en route. Praise the Lord!"

APPLICATION

Of course, not all storms have such a rainbow ending. But take comfort in the fact that—in the midst of the storm, in the midst of war, in the midst of hatred—calm is approaching. Trouble does not last always. If you submit to the perfect will of Christ, you will have peace in knowing that God has your best interests at heart. In the words of Jesus, "These things have I spoken unto you, that in me ye might have peace. In the world ye shall have tribulation: but be of good cheer; I have overcome the world" (John 16:33).

The next time your problems cause you to lose sleep, speak these words to your spirit: "I will both lay me down in peace, and sleep: for thou, Lord, only makest me dwell in safety" (Psalm 4:8). If you still cannot sleep, get up and read your Bible or select a devotional tape that reminds you that you are in the arms of God.

PRAYER

Lord, I know that You are with me and everywhere at all times. I ask that You grant me Your perfect peace. In the name of Jesus, I pray. Amen.

OCTOBER

WEEK FIVE: SELF-CONTROL

DAY 1 / REWIND

CONTROL YOURSELF...

"What fruit had ye then in those things whereof ye are now ashamed? for the end of those things is death."

Romans 6:21

Lindsay owned a large, expensively furnished townhouse. Her career as a corporate communications specialist was paying off, and then she met the man of her dreams.

After they'd been dating regularly for eight months, she was convinced he would be her future husband. He said all the right things. They did all the right things together—attending church and weekly Bible study, praying, and reading Scripture. She thought they were a match made in heaven.

Then he became distant. Lindsay could not figure out what was wrong. She honored his request for "space" to ponder their future. What she thought would be a few days turned into a month. And then late one night as she sat in her living room unable to sleep and staring out the window, she realized she saw his car parked outside a townhouse directly across from hers.

She had to find out if she was dreaming and grabbed her robe, locked the door, and headed across the parking lot. That was definitely his car; she recognized the decorative sticker she'd bought him recently. She rang the neighbor's doorbell. When the door opened, she stormed in and found him sitting in the family room. Before he could react or she could stop herself, she hit him in the nose with the base of her palm, spun away, and marched back home.

APPLICATION

In Romans 6:15, the apostle Paul asks the saints, "What then? Shall we sin because we are not under law but under grace? By no means!" (NIV). Jesus was crucified and died on the Cross as a ransom for our sins. Our old selves were crucified with Him so that the sinful body might be destroyed. In order to consider ourselves alive with Christ, we must be willing to die to sin. When we yield to anger, violence, fear, deceit, or betrayal, we are slaves to sin. We can choose to yield to sin or choose to yield to the fruit of the Spirit, which includes self-control. Self-control is a choice. Paul instructs us to exercise self-control with the same zeal that we had when we yielded our bodies to sin. The wages of sin is death, but the free gift of God is eternal life.

Think of a situation in your life where you did not exercise self-control. What reward did you get from your sin? In your journal, write what happened and how you responded. Then REWIND. Instead of what you did, write what you wish you'd done. In what ways does this wish reflect more accurately the teachings of the apostle Paul and the character of Jesus? How might your actions and words show the fruitfulness of self-control?

PRAYER

Dear God, please forgive me for allowing my emotions to run amok. Lord, I know You and I are in control of me. No matter how poorly another person treats me, I always have the power to resist losing control because I can do all things through Christ who strengthens me. Let this Scripture and the teachings in this chapter become manifest in my spirit so that I will exercise self-control and respond with the character of Jesus Christ. Amen.

DAY 2 / SIT DOWN, SHUT YOUR MOUTH, AND HOLD ON!

CONTROL YOUR TONGUE...

"Even so the tongue is a little member, and boasteth great things. Behold, how great a matter a little fire kindleth!"

James 3:5

Vanessa and Mark had only been married 18 months, but it was not working out. Mark was much stricter with money than Vanessa was; and when she maxed out a credit card, he put her on a budget. In response, Vanessa packed up her belongings and moved into a friend's spare bedroom. As she was unpacking, Vanessa discovered she'd taken some personal items of Mark's—childhood photos, cards, and letters. She called his cell phone and left a message asking if he wanted to pick the items up. Mark returned the call, leaving a message on Vanessa's cell phone and asking her to mail the items to him.

Mark was stunned when he checked his voice mail the next day. Vanessa told him that she didn't care that he didn't want see her; she didn't want to see him either. She said she had no intention of paying the expense of mailing his junk back to him. She called him several insulting names such as "childish" and "ugly" and told him she'd decided to burn his photographs, cards, and letters.

Instead of responding immediately, Mark spent hours digesting Vanessa's response. Then he left her another message. "The reason I asked you to mail the materials to me is because I'm not able to pick them up. I'm in New Orleans with my dad, who is ill. Please go by the house and put the stuff in my mailbox. Take care of yourself."

APPLICATION

In James 3, we read about the tongue. The tongue is a small part of the body, but the damage it can cause can be astronomical, almost insurmountable. James describes the tongue as a fire. From the same mouth can come blessing and cursing. But for the children of God this ought not to occur. Instead, James recommends that we sow goodness and meekness of wisdom. That's what Mark did in the story above. The harvest of righteousness is sown in peace for everyone who chooses to make peace with others.

Can you refrain from giving someone "a piece of your mind" the way Vanessa let her tongue control her attitude? The next time anyone says or does something hurtful to you, take six hours to pray and meditate before you respond. Continue to increase the response time until you can go 24 hours before responding. Exhibiting wisdom that is pure, peaceable, gentle, and sincere will start to mean more to you than the instant gratification of retaliation.

PRAYER

Dear God, I can't imagine not responding immediately to painful things people say and do to me. My human response is a desire to inflict greater pain. Help me to remember and demonstrate the wisdom highlighted in James 3—pure, peaceable, gentle, merciful, sincere wisdom—so that my example mirrors the righteousness of Christ. Amen.

DAY 3 / YOUR HONOR

CONTROL THE URGE FOR REVENGE...

"Be kindly affectioned one to another with brotherly love; in honour preferring one another."
Romans 12:10

Madeline and Myra, inseparable since high school, attended the same college and were roommates. They trusted each other wholeheartedly. When sophomore year started, Madeline met William in chemistry class. Myra was very happy for Madeline as she listened to her friend describing William's kindness and honesty. And when she met him, Myra knew immediately why Madeline admired him so.

Sometimes, when his classes ended for the day, William headed to the girls' room to wait for Madeline. Madeline thought it was a great arrangement. Then, at the end of junior year, Myra and William told Madeline the truth. They had gotten sexually intimate and Myra was pregnant. They got an apartment and moved in together.

Two years later, Madeline was in a coffee shop when she heard William's voice. She'd hoped her feelings for him had died; she hadn't seen or spoken to him or Myra in two years. William told her he still loved her and wanted them to reunite. "Myra never has to know," he insisted.

Madeline thought about Myra and little William. She wondered if she could regain the happiness she'd felt. They agreed to meet again the next day.

William was all smiles the next day when he approached Madeline in the coffee shop. Madeline was smiling, too, as she told William that although she still had feelings for him, she preferred not to do to Myra what Myra and William had done to her. She wished him the best and walked confidently away.

APPLICATION

In Romans 12:10-19, Paul encourages the Romans to present themselves blemish-free unto the Lord and to remember that it is reasonable to do so. After all that God has done for us by sending His Son to atone for our sins, the minimum we should offer in return is to be a living sacrifice. Paul further instructs that we not return evil behavior with evil actions of our own. Instead, we should do what is honest and live peaceably with our brothers and sisters. Paul tells us not to attempt to be vengeful but to leave wrath and vengeance in God's hands (Deuteronomy 32:35; Romans 12:19). In other words, control the temptation—don't even think about getting even! Let it go!

What is your response when a retaliatory opportunity presents itself? Think about a person or situation that is so distressing that you have refused to think about it. A friend betrayed you. Your supervisor fired or demoted you. Your spouse deceived or abandoned you. Start praying for that person today. Pray that God will be gracious and merciful toward the person. Initially, this will be a grueling exercise and you might not feel sincere in your prayers. Be honest with God; He already knows how you feel. But each day your capacity to pray sincerely will increase, so that when your enemies are thirsty and hungry, you will give them food and water.

PRAYER

Dear God, I know Jesus was mocked and scourged for our transgressions, but He did not return evil for evil. I endeavor to be more honorable than those who spitefully use me. Increase my desire and my capacity for self-control so that I do not conform to the ways of this world by getting even, but instead overcome evil by doing good in the likeness of Your Son, Jesus Christ. Amen.

DAY 4 / REPUTATION OR CHARACTER?

CONTROL YOUR AMBITION...

"I have not sat with vain persons, neither will I go in with dissemblers."
Psalm 26:4

Recently, Barbara joined her church's singles ministry. She really admired the co-chairs, Sharon and Claudia. They were very knowledgeable about the Scriptures. In addition, they were extremely popular with the church's pastor, deacons, and trustees, who included them in important meetings. Unexpectedly for Barbara, Sharon and Claudia began increasing her contribution: They asked her to help develop packets for singles ministry meetings; and they included her on the agenda, asking her to read the Scripture or say a prayer. Barbara was proud to be associated with the two women.

After one of the ministry meetings, Sharon and Claudia invited Barbara to Claudia's place. Barbara was honored. She expected the conversation to be more personal, but she got more than she bargained for. Sharon and Claudia started gossiping. They said the leader of the couples ministry disrespected his wife. Some of the singles ministry members had confessed to Sharon that they were sexually intimate. And there was an affair going on between a choir member and a married man. Claudia and Sharon laughed as they talked about all the happenings between congregants.

Barbara's head was spinning. Although she was tempted to go along with the pair, she asked to leave. She needed time to think things over. At home, when she had time to reflect, she realized that Sharon and Claudia were leading double lives. She ceased contact with them and began attending the seniors ministry instead, finding its leaders' integrity more compatible with hers.

APPLICATION

How easy it is for a woman to choose to be popular at the expense of her relationship with God! Psalm 26 is David's affirmation of his integrity and a prayer that God would be cognizant of his choice. That's what self-control is—a choice, a decision to do what is right even when you are tempted not to. James 4:17 says, "If anyone, then, knows the good they ought to do and doesn't do it, it is sin for them" (NIV). Or in the words of my late grandfather, "If you know better, you ought to do better."

What do you stand for? Do people know? Are any of your religious friends or acquaintances comfortable with relaxing God's commandments, and do they encourage you to do the same? Are you prepared to separate yourself from them? Will you start today?

PRAYER

Dear God, forgive me for allowing dissemblers to invade my relationship with You. While I understand that Jesus walked among sinners, He never violated Your commandments. He immediately acknowledged and rebuked evil when it was displayed in His presence. Help me to choose a walk of integrity with You that demonstrates my appreciation for self-control rather than my desire for popularity. Amen.

CONTROL YOUR FINANCES...

"When thou goest, thy steps shall not be straitened; and when thou runnest, thou shalt not stumble."

Proverbs 4:12

When Kara began attending Cornell University on a full scholarship, it was her first time living on her own. Although Kara's mother had taught her many aspects of life, other decisions awaited. Kara hated riding the bus. Instead of buying books, she paid for a down payment on a car and figured she'd borrow books. Then credit card applications came in the mail. Kara decided a credit card could pay for gas and car upkeep. As soon as the card arrived, she drove to New York City and shopped.

The next semester, she didn't buy books or a meal plan on campus. The money her mom sent her didn't cover payments for her three credit cards. She wasn't sure how she'd gotten so many cards, but she realized suddenly that she owed thousands of dollars. She got a job. But her grades dropped and the university notified her that she'd forfeit her scholarship if her grades didn't improve. Mortified, she called her mother and confessed.

"Grab your Bible," her mother instructed. Her mother read Matthew 6:19-34 and said, "None of the stuff you've collected really matters because God knows what you need and will provide for you. You must learn to wait until you can afford the things you want."

Kara's mother explained how to contact creditors, relinquish the credit cards, and get back on the right track. Kara sold the car and used the free campus buses. Eventually, she graduated with honors and debt-free!

APPLICATION

The book of Proverbs contains moral and ethical instructions dealing with many aspects of life, especially self-control. It tells you that you will not lack what you need for daily existence. As you continue on the path of life, you will not stumble and fall if you are grounded and rooted in wisdom. When we are fulfilled spiritually, we will not feel cheated if we do not have everything we want. We will not feel so driven to buy and achieve and grasp if we have already grasped the gift of eternal life and a relationship with Christ. Money pales in comparison with the riches of grace; and as we apply this fruit of the Holy Spirit to our daily routines, it enriches us immeasurably.

What's in your wallet? Do you spend your time and money on acquiring more things? How much do you spend getting to know God? Study Luke 18:18-29, reading these verses a few times as you consider how the passage relates to self-control. How do these verses speak to you in terms of your tendencies? The next time you find yourself on the verge of losing control over your spending habits, ask Jesus to enrich your capability for self-control so you can acquire more wisdom. You can never spend too much time investing in God and how to apply His Word to your life.

PRAYER

Dear God, I'm guilty of neglecting You, my family, and friends because I spend too much time working to pay for all the stuff I've been collecting, the things that make me popular. Inspire me instead to seek wisdom, which will increase my capacity to control my spending. The more I know about You, the easier it will be for me to live within my means. Amen.

NOVEMBER

WEEK ONE: GOD'S WORD IS YEA AND NAY

DAY 1 / ALL PROMISES, NOT JUST A FEW

YOU CAN SHOUT NOW!

"For all the promises of God in him are yea, and in him Amen, unto the glory of God by us."
2 Corinthians 1:20

Lorina was leading the monthly meeting of the Chosen, a ministry group at her church, when Janis said, "I'm tired of buying things that don't work."

Lorina asked, "What do you mean?"

"I purchased some software that hasn't done as the manufacturer promised. It seems that not only the things I buy, but also a lot of the people I know, promise one thing and do something else."

Lorina said, "It often seems that people make promises and don't keep them."

"I guess I just have to learn to accept it because that's the way life is." Janis sighed.

Quickly Lorina responded, "I don't agree that we have to accept it." Others in the group joined the conversation.

"You can trust your family," someone said, but that statement was challenged by a member who had been betrayed by a relative.

"You can trust a Christian," another asserted.

Someone else whispered, "Not all the time."

Finally, a quiet voice said, "You can trust God and God's promises."

Several people in the group chimed in, "Thank God for that!"

APPLICATION

In today's Scripture, Paul clarifies the idea of promises and faithfulness. With God, there is no such thing as saying "yes" and then meaning "no," Paul tells us. With God, because of His gift of His only Son, a promise is the equivalent of "yes, yes"—or "yes" with a giant exclamation mark and an "Amen" to top it off. Paul also pointed out that he was not being indecisive when he changed the timing of his visit to Corinth. He wanted the believers in Corinth to become more unified so that the focus of his time could be on spreading joy.

This week, search the Bible for examples of God's promises. Choose one promise from God and pray it every day. Read the promise by placing your name in front of it as if God spoke it directly to you—which of course, He did.

PRAYER

God, help me to remember today that You are the original promise keeper and that all Your promises are "yes, yes" and "Amen." I am thankful for Your Word. Amen.

DAY 2 / KNOW THE PROMISE MAKER

WOMAN OF GOD, YOU CAN STAND ON THIS...

"For I know the thoughts that I think toward you, saith the Lord, thoughts of peace, and not of evil, to give you an expected end."
Jeremiah 29:11

One day, Jessica and Jermani found a bracelet. "Look, Jessica, this bracelet has letters. What do they say?" asked Jermani who was nearly five years old and learning the alphabet.

Jessica was eight and could read. "F- R-O-G, frog," she answered.

Jermani knew that frogs hopped a lot. She hopped the rest of the way home with Jessica.

When they got home, they showed their grandmother the bracelet. Grandma said, "Yes, it does say that, but this stands for more than just frog."

Jessica looked puzzled. "But it says F-R-O-G and that spells frog."

Their grandmother said, "Yes, but look closely and tell me what you see after each letter." Jessica looked again and said, "F-period, R-period, O-period, G-period."

Her grandmother smiled. "That's right. Do you know what the period means?"

"No," said Jessica and Jermani.

Her grandmother continued, "The period means each letter stands for a whole word. The letters stand for Fully Rely On God."

Jessica and Jermani took the bracelet and said, "Fully Rely On God." With that, they ran off to share with their friends what F.R.O.G. really means.

APPLICATION

When we know the promises of God, they become words that we can stand on because they will last. "The earth is the Lord's, and the fullness thereof; the world, and they who dwell therein" reminds us that God is in control (Psalm 24:1). We also can be thankful for the Word, which tells us that we have new, eternal life in Christ. When you fully rely on God, His teachings empower you so you can share His blessings.

Today, whenever a need arises that indicates an emerging doubt, stand on one of God's promises. Use the list of Scriptures from last week or add more examples. Remember to thank God for His unchanging promise keeping.

PRAYER

God, help me to fully rely on You. I will stand on Your Word and remember that in You I have the abundant assurance of every promise. In Jesus' name, I pray. Amen.

DAY 3 / HOLDING ONTO THE PROMISE

WHEN IT DOESN'T LOOK LIKE, FEEL LIKE, OR SMELL LIKE "YES"...

"Therefore, brethren, stand fast, and hold the traditions which ye have been taught, whether by word, or our epistle."
2 Thessalonians 2:15

"Well, I tried that faith thing and it has not worked," Muriel said to her minister. "When I first got sick, I thought I heard God whisper to me that this sickness wasn't until death. But I'm still sick." Tears formed in her dark eyes.

Pastor Smith ducked into her office and came back with some seeds in her hand. "Muriel, if you have correctly understood God's promise, then you can hold onto that promise. Take these mustard seeds as a reminder that this is all the faith you need."

It took a long time, but slowly Muriel got stronger. One Sunday at testimony time, she stood and said, "Maybe somebody is here today ready to give up; but if God has said He will do something for you or that something will happen in your life, you can believe God. Even when it doesn't seem like it, God is working it out for His glory."

APPLICATION

Sometimes it seems that everyone around you is being blessed and that God is so busy answering other people's needs that He has forgotten about you. The enemy of our soul enters our weariness and whispers that God has forgotten us or given up on us. When we feel that way, it's quite a challenge to be thankful. But God is still at work. We just need to wait on Him.

Look at some mustard seeds (in the spice section). Notice how small the seeds are. Read the parable of the mustard seed (Mark 4:30-34). Consider the parable's meaning in relation to being thankful when a test of faith exists. Say, "God, I will believe today that You will fulfill that which You have promised." Then every day, repeat the statement. How does the experience of restating your faith affect your sense of gratitude?

PRAYER

God, I confess that there have been times when I doubted that You would fulfill Your promises to me. Forgive me, Lord, and help me to believe that You are working on my behalf. Amen.

DAY 4 / WALK IN THE PROMISE

SO BE IT...

"And so, after he had patiently endured, he obtained the promise."
Hebrews 6:15

Two women who volunteered to get the church decorated the day before the pastor's anniversary service were talking in the sanctuary.

One of the women said, "There's a lot to get done."

"How are we going to get all this work accomplished?" said the other. She counted off tasks: dusting the pews and vacuuming the floor and polishing the altar. Then the potted plants needed to be set along the altar, flowers needed to be cut and placed inside vases, and the programs needed to be unpacked from the cartons. She was sure they would be there until quite late.

"To be truthful, I really don't know how we'll do it," said the other volunteer. "I just believe that things will work out."

They started working. In came a sister who said she could help for a few minutes. Then in came the pastor's wife who said she was glad to lend a hand. A few others appeared and helped, too. The women finished the last of the tasks and thanked everyone for coming. They headed home, laughing together: God had promised to help and He did.

APPLICATION

Sometimes God calls us to walk out His promises as if they are already fulfilled. We sometimes are called to move forward believing that God will work it out. When we reach the point of fulfillment—when we can see some of the evidence we could not picture before—we can experience the lightening of our burden and the pleasure of gratitude.

To help the Scripture become real to you today, create a little song to help you remember Hebrews 6:15. As you go through the day singing your newly created song, the meaning will get inside of you and help you to remember that God's promises are true.

PRAYER

"Amen, so be it." These are words of assurance and hope. We thank You for this complete assurance. Help us to hear Your "amen" and to have the assurance that it will be so because You have decreed it. Amen.

DAY 5 / PROMISES FULFILLED

THE OTHER SIDE OF THROUGH

"And blessed is she that believed: for there shall be a performance of those things which were told her from the Lord."

Luke 1:45

There was so much enthusiasm as each woman came through the door at the event that signified their completion of pastorate studies. Marilyn, Sandy, Janet, Bernadette, Dorothy, Delrio, and Natalie had shared the journey; and they were excited about all that God had done. The air was electrified as each of them stood and told everyone in the audience about their experience. There were days when it seemed the promises would not be fulfilled. In testimony after testimony, they added, "But God was with me" or "God kept me and didn't let me go."

It was truly a Holy Ghost party that just couldn't stop. The women's journeys to pastorates had been long and hard. But now, with praise on their lips and a dance in their feet, they honored God with what God had choreographed just for them. Out of joy and gratitude, they danced and sang for all the promises that had come true.

APPLICATION

After the Children of Israel crossed the Red Sea, Miriam led the women in a special song and dance (Exodus 15:1-21). Perhaps as they danced, they looked back and remembered all the babies that had been killed, the bricks made without straw, the days when they thought they wouldn't make it, when they thought that God had forgotten His promise to them. Life includes difficult seasons, but there are seasons of joy, too. Hold on to the promise because you will be able to shout and dance your thankfulness on the other side. Today, ask God to give you a new mind and a new attitude so you can live on the other side of your problems with freedom and joy.

PRAYER

God, I thank You that You have been faithful to keep every promise and that every word You have spoken has come true. God, in the fullness of Your time, You bring me from one place to another. Thanks, God, for bringing me through. Amen.

WEEK TWO: COMMITMENT TO COMMUNITY

DAY 1 / A KNOCK FOR KIYANA

LOVE THAT NEIGHBOR OF MINE?

"And the second is like unto it, Thou shalt love thy neighbour as thyself."
Matthew 22:39

The knock at her door was very surprising to Sharon, especially given the late hour. She walked to the door, shushing her barking dog. "Who is it?" she called out.

A woman answered, "Hi. My name is Valerie. I live right behind you. Have you seen my daughter, Kiyana?"

Sharon flung the door open at the sound of her neighbor's quivering voice.

"No, sorry, I've been inside all evening."

"I told her a million times to stay in the house until I get home from work." Tears spilled down Valerie's face. "I've got to go."

Sharon scribbled her phone number on a notepad and Valerie took the paper, nodding distractedly as she went outside. Sharon closed the door and leaned against it. Then she attached the dog's leash to him, grabbed her jacket and keys, and headed outside. It was bad enough she didn't even know Valerie and Kiyana. The least she could do was help her next door neighbor.

APPLICATION

Jesus Christ singles out the two great commandments ever given to humankind: 1) to love God with all of your heart, mind, and soul; and 2) to love your neighbor as yourself. Our Lord's second greatest commandment is not always easy to live up to, is it? Everyone you encounter is your neighbor. There's no better time than right now to begin doing what God commanded; and when we love neighbors as God loves us and as we aspire to love ourselves, we experience a higher form of love.

Be kind to at least one neighbor a day for the next five days. Compliment people, thank them, let other drivers merge in front of you, and express your kindness in as many ways as possible. Pray to God that He helps you become the best neighbor you can possibly be.

PRAYER

Help me, dear God, to obey Your commandment to love my neighbor as myself. Fill me with a loving and tender heart. I pray that my words and actions show a full commitment to my community. Amen.

THE NEIGHBORHOOD CORNER SCHOOL...

"Get wisdom, get understanding: forget it not; neither decline from the words of my mouth. Forsake her not, and she shall preserve thee: love her, and she shall keep thee. Wisdom is the principal thing; therefore get wisdom: and with all thy getting get understanding. Exalt her, and she shall promote thee: she shall bring thee to honour, when thou dost embrace her. She shall give to thine head an ornament of grace: a crown of glory shall she deliver to thee.

Proverbs 4:5-9

Janine had a lot to be thankful for. Here she was, a new graduate of Howard University. Seven years had passed of being in and out of foster care, sometimes on the streets of New York City as a runaway, but now she was a mature young lady with her focus squarely on God. Janine had two teachers and two pastors to thank for supporting her efforts and praying for her during tumult and tribulation. She was really glad that all four were able to attend her graduation from college.

After the ceremony, the four adults who'd been helped her achieve a bachelor's degree took her to dinner. She picked a seafood place in D.C. that she'd often walked by but hadn't been able to afford before. As she sat at a table with Ms. Walker, Mr. Brown, and Pastors

Grace and Tim Martin, Janine said, "Let's hold hands and bow our heads." She led her community of special people in a prayer of thanks.

APPLICATION

As was the case with Janine in today's story, children need adults' caring and expertise to become wholesome grown-ups. In subtle and obvious ways, your compassionate contribution to the life of children in your community can be a major factor in their fate.

Consider how you might help with children's development. These include: tutoring in an after school program, assisting with a Sunday school class, donating supplies for a Bible camp, etc. If you prefer to help with adult learning, locate a literacy program or continuing education class—when adults improve their education, they often become better parents. Or increase your own knowledge with a class or workshop. Ask the Lord to bless the path of education.

PRAYER

Dear Father, thank You for giving me the tools I need in order to learn and encourage others' education. Give me the strength and courage, dear Lord, to live a life full of wisdom. Amen.

DAY 3 / DENISE'S J.O.B.

THE NEIGHBORHOOD MALL...

"Therefore take no thought, saying, What shall we eat? or, What shall we drink? or, Wherewithal shall we be clothed? (For after all these things do the Gentiles seek:) for your heavenly Father knoweth that ye have need of all these things. But seek ye first the kingdom of God, and his righteousness; and all these things shall be added unto you."

Matthew 6:31-33

Denise wanted to have her own successful business. She opened a store making and selling African dolls. The store was a small but clean, orderly location in an African American neighborhood, and she employed a few teens and young adult residents of the community. However, her sales rarely increased beyond four dolls a week. Nevertheless, she stayed on her knees begging God not to let her yield to thoughts of imminent failure.

After increasing her efforts to market her dolls, expenses increased but sales decreased. The phrase "get a real job" filled her ears. Denise spent more time in prayer, seeking the Lord's direction. She also thanked God in advance for providing comfort and support. Gradually, her shop began getting more customers and selling more dolls. She hired more employees and expanded her location. Today, Denise's two-story building employs dozens and houses the largest-selling African doll company in Georgia.

APPLICATION

If your community has new, burgeoning business development, then you are part of a community that supports its business owners. Thriving businesses create jobs and wealth within neighborhoods. Like most people, you want restaurants, shopping, and other resources nearby because these enterprises support property values and your quality of life. Invest in your community by supporting its local businesses.

Find one business in your neighborhood that is succeeding and one that looks useful but needs uplift. Ask at your church for ways that congregants can support both businesses. Pray that God's will be done with business development in your community. Have a prayer at church that the Lord helps the entire congregation to become a vehicle for business growth in your neighborhood.

PRAYER

Dear Father, thank You for increasing my sense of what it means to be part of a community. Dear Lord, help me and everyone in my community to achieve an attitude of success and victory, and to defeat thoughts of failure and defeat. Amen.

DAY 4 / A RAY OF HOPE WHEN YOU NEED IT MOST
THE NEIGHBORHOOD CHURCH...

"Then shall he answer them, saying, Verily I say unto you, Inasmuch as
ye did it not to one of the least of these, ye did it not to me."
Matthew 25:45

Alicia's House was a church-funded place that sheltered and supported women and their children while the women made a transition into self-sufficiency. Most of the women at Alicia's House were Christian. Vernatta had been a faithful congregant but had stopped going. When her husband left her their two kids, a dog, and a pile of bills, she decided she didn't have the time, energy, money, or willingness to attend church. It had seemed to her that there wasn't anything to be thankful for, so why bother with church?

Her mind began to change, though, while she stayed at Alicia's House. The workers helped her find a job and training that would improve her employability. The Christian women at the house volunteered to watch her kids (for free) after school. Without that offer, Janice probably would have lost her job and the training course. She told the women that she'd almost given up hope that things were ever get better. She'd done everything in her power to make things right. She wanted to work and tried hard to raise her kids properly.

Vernatta hugged her friends and said, "And now I have all of you helping me. Ladies, you are my ray of hope. First chance I get, I'll help you in any way I can. Thank you."

APPLICATION

The church in any community should be a shining beacon to all its neighbors. Today, millions of children have nowhere to go after school. Mothers worry about their children's safety while they are at work. Most crimes committed by or against kids occur on weekdays between 3:00 p.m. and 6:00 p.m. When churches open their doors to schoolchildren, we fulfill the community's basic needs—and this is a true testimony to the love of God.

Find out if the youth ministry in your church has an after school program. If not, ask your pastor or youth ministry leader to consider allowing the church to serve the needs of children after school. If your church already has an after school program, consider lending a hand or donating supplies.

PRAYER

Our Father who art in heaven, just as You watch over us every moment of our lives, give us here on earth the passion to do the same. Our children need watchful, caring eyes upon them all the time. Give us the wisdom and courage to open our doors to those in need. Amen.

DAY 5 / LEAVING THE NEIGHBORHOOD

I THOUGHT WE WERE MOVIN' ON UP...

"His lord said unto him, Well done, thou good and faithful servant: thou hast been faithful over a few things, I will make thee ruler over many things: enter thou into the joy of thy lord."
Matthew 25:21

"This is a nice neighborhood," Edwina Peterson told her agent. "I put a lot of money into this house. It's worth $250,000."

Her agent Andrea Sutter said, "Your house has been up for sale for over five months. This the first time anyone has offered you more than $199,000 for it."

Edwina Peterson sipped tea and looked out of her kitchen window at her backyard's neat lawn, pretty garden, flagstone patio, outdoor furniture, and outdoor kitchen. She and her husband Terrance sacrificed vacations and new cars to pay for all that, and they'd renovated the kitchen and bathrooms as well. They liked the neighborhood. She and Terrance raised three kids here, and now—with Terrance passed on and the kids grown and in other cities—it was time to downsize.

She shrugged. It wasn't the best time to move on, but it was understandable while she still had her health and a job. She'd find a small place near her daughter. This community

113

had been good to her and her family. Maybe the buyers would help keep this community good. She put down her mug of tea and said, "I'll accept it."

APPLICATION

A bad economy can turn hard-earned investments into losses. Even in neighborhoods where residents keep their homes well-maintained and businesses and churches do likewise, an entire community can experience decline.

Rather than sitting around immersed in depression and self-pity, there are things we can do. Make sure your own home and surrounding area are clean, inside and out. Use your church and neighborhood organizations to organize regular neighborhood cleanup days. Block by block, send outreach teams to get people involved in proactive caretaking of the community. Pray for the Lord to move your neighbors' hearts to show their pride in a healthy, clean community that reflects His glory.

PRAYER

Dear Lord, You are perfectly pure. I pray for Your help, dear Lord, in reflecting Your character of cleanliness and order in my home and in my community. Amen.

WEEK THREE: FRIENDSHIP

DAY 1 / WHAT DOES IT REALLY MEAN?

A FRIEND INDEED...

"Iron sharpeneth iron; so a man sharpeneth the countenance of his friend."
Proverbs 27:17

My job as an emergency room nurse is pretty intense and requires the ability to quickly assess situations and then help others make decisions—decisions that can have a big impact on someone's life. Therefore, everyone teamed up with me has to have excellent skills and alertness. We encounter trauma on a daily, sometimes hourly, basis. From the intake clerks to the doctors and the rest of the team, we must remain sharp yet sensitive, smart about every possible medical diagnosis, yet aware that we are treating human beings who are suffering and need compassionate care.

Most of us are friends—I guess because we know each other well and like working together. We count on each other's expertise, and we depend on one another to be at our top level of performance for several hours at a stretch no matter how tough things get. When my shift ends, I go home, hug my husband and kids, and get on my knees so I can thank God for His watchful care and love for me and my friends.

APPLICATION

Identifying the best qualities of a friend should be the first step in determining whether or not you have one. Your best resource is the Bible. The Word of God tells us that a friend: acts as your intercessor (Job 16:20, NIV), will bring out the best in you and provide it in kind (Proverbs 27:17), and is there to help you up when difficulties cause you to waver (Ecclesiastes 4:10). As today's story shows us, the epitome of friendship involves utter trust in each other's highest level of effort, as was the case with David and Jonathan in 1 Samuel 20. If you find yourself in need of a true-blue friend, wouldn't it be best to feel complete confidence in the person?

Take a moment to think about your relationships. Are your friends there for you during times of trouble? Do they intercede for you when you are going through a storm in life? Have they brought something to the relationship that has helped build your spiritual growth? If the answer is yes, praise God that He has allowed you to experience the true meaning of a friend. If the answer is no, pray that God will bless you with a friend that is defined by His Word.

PRAYER

Lord, I thank You for letting me know what a friend really is. Give me the wisdom and discernment to know friend from foe and help me to understand how I can serve as a good friend. Thank You, Lord, for the blessing of friendship. Amen.

DAY 2 / THAT'S MY FINAL ANSWER!
WHAT A FRIEND WE HAVE IN JESUS...

"Know ye not that the friendship of the world is enmity with God?
whosoever therefore will be a friend of the world is the enemy of God."
James 4:4b

I used to hang out with some seriously committed partiers. I spent every Saturday with a group of young people and thought of them as my friends. We took pride in getting home close to sunrise on Sundays. Go to church? No, we nursed hangovers on Sundays, slowly pulling ourselves together in time to make it to work on Mondays.

I defined friendship through the filter of carefree drinking, dancing, and club-hopping. For many years, I thought this was the way to live. I didn't know this kind of friendship meant I was an enemy of the Lord's. After a while, though, I got bored. A coworker persuaded me to attend church with her. "Just once and you'll begin to feel different," she said. Turns out she was right.

I have learned that God desires to be my friend. I have learned to call on Him when I become nervous or afraid or I just need His support and loving care. I've come to know this because He has helped me when I didn't even want Him to. So if someone were to ask me, "Who do you love?" My response is: "Jesus, and that's my final answer!"

APPLICATION

Always remember that regardless of what you may experience in life, God's Word is true; and He will never leave you or forsake you because He is your best friend always. God longs for you to let Him be your best friend, but He won't force it. The choice is yours. What is your final answer?

Are you still partying with the world on Saturday and lazily praising God on Sunday? Consider how your incomplete commitment is affecting your relationship with Him. Schedule your time on Saturday in such a way that Sunday becomes the highlight of your weekend. Repeat this undertaking for an entire month; then write a note to yourself that describes how you feel about your new best friend, the Lord.

PRAYER

Lord, I thank You for bringing me into greater awareness of friendship. I will boldly declare my friendship with You and make our connection my top priority. I love You, my Lord. Amen.

DAY 3 / WHAT AN INTRODUCTION!

YOU'RE GETTING BEHIND THE RIGHT ONE...

"Henceforth I call you not servants; for the servant knoweth not what his lord doeth: but I have called you friends."

John 15:15a

Imagine being at a huge social gathering of thousands of people. As you are walking around, you recognize some of the people but not many. People are staring at you because they notice that you are following the host. Many are calling you a follower, but you are happy following the host. People are watching, talking, and wondering about you and your connection to the host. Silence overtakes the room as the host approaches the microphone.

"Hello, everyone, my name is Jesus," the host says and as He points to you, He says, "This is My friend."

APPLICATION

Think about your best friend. You feel you can talk to your best friend about anything. You trust and depend on your best friend. As positive as that relationship may be, it cannot compare to friendship with the Lord because your close friend has human limitations.

Friends can help you when you're hurting, but only God can heal you completely. That doesn't mean that you don't have good friends; it proves that God is more than a friend.

Form a mental picture of God introducing you as His friend. Throughout the many times you have been introduced to people, do any of these occasions compare to your visualization of hearing God say, "This is My friend"? When people spread rumors about you or call you ungodly names, keep your head up knowing that God calls you friend, and He is never too busy to listen.

PRAYER

Lord, thank You for Your friendship. I am grateful that my friendship with You doesn't depend on how great I may think I am but on how great I know that You are. Amen.

DAY 4 / A LETTER TO MY FRIEND

WHO TREATS YOU BETTER THAN YOU TREAT HIM?

"There is a friend that sticketh closer than a brother."
Proverbs 18:24b

A powerful sense of thankfulness awakened her, and she knew she had to write a message right away. She rose, went to her desk, and began a letter she needed to write.

Dear Lord: You were there in the beginning and I know you'll be there in the end too—guiding me, instructing me, correcting me, and telling me what I should do.

You comforted me as I wept on more than one night. You reassured me, and I always felt Your presence right beside me. There have been times when peace, joy, and happiness were too far away. But You said, "Let Me fight this battle; I guarantee you I'll win." So I turned it over to You, and now I feel joy emerging in me.

As I write this letter, I can feel myself smiling. That's because I'm thinking of You, Lord, and I know that You will always be my friend.

APPLICATION

God has always been with you, throughout every situation. He is a friend like none other. God has never left you because He is your Lord, your God, and your friend. Every person you meet will always have the potential for being imperfect at friendship. Not God; you can depend completely on Him for continuous, wholehearted friendship.

Write a letter to God. Tell Him what it means to you to be called His friend. Thank Him for what He has done in your life, and praise Him for what is yet to come.

PRAYER

Lord, I thank You for being there when no one else was there for me. Thank You for Your immeasurable and incomparable friendship. I am blessed to know that I have a friend, and His name is Jesus. Amen.

DAY 5 / THAT'S MY FRIEND!

AT ALL TIMES...

"A friend loveth at all times, and a brother is born for adversity."
Proverbs 17:17

Privacy and freedom are two of the many benefits to having a best friend. You entrust subjects to your best friend that you would be hard-pressed to reveal to anyone else. You both express yourselves at a depth of emotion and experience that reflects your willingness to "go there" because you feel free from judgmental reactions or gossip. In addition, best friends provide mutuality: Each will give back what the other receives.

Your friendship is about more than just a good time. You share values; for both of you, God is number one in everything you do and you both respect His place in your lives. When one of you experiences something that bolsters your relationship with God—such as a song or a ministry—you share this because it reinforces your friendship while strengthening each of you. Although busy schedules prevent you from spending time together, both of you have confidence and love for one another, which enables you to wait expectantly for the next wonderful time together. You thank God for your trustworthy, authentic friendship. You thank God for your best friend.

APPLICATION

Close friends are rare, and it's a blessing to have one special friend. It's equally special to provide the level of friendship described above. When two people plant a seed of friendship, each person must nurture it with love, time, support, encouragement, and truth, and then watch it grow.

Don't take your friend for granted. As soon as you can, call or write her and tell her how much she has blessed you. Make this the moment when you let her know you feel blessed to understand true friendship because of her.

PRAYER

Lord, I thank You for sending me my close friend. I thank You for helping me show how I can be someone's close friend. Thank You for being my example of the perfect friend. Amen.

DAY 1 / THANK YOU FOR TODAY, LORD
TOMORROW'S TOO TOUGH FOR ME!

"Take therefore no thought for the morrow: for the morrow shall take thought for the things of itself."

Matthew 6:34a

Anika stepped aside as her sister Marquetta added rolls and butter to the table. They were having a feast. Eight chairs surrounded the table—five more than she, Marquetta, and Aunt Viola usually had for dinner.

It had started with Marquetta's announcement that she invited two friends from college to Thanksgiving dinner. Aunt Viola agreed that no one should spend a holiday away from home, eating junk food.

Then Anika thought of the Carter sisters, who had recently moved into their apartment building. "Could they come, too?" she asked.

Aunt Viola told her this was a wonderful idea; and while they were at it, Mr. Forrest from upstairs was always doing favors for them—maybe he'd be their fifth guest.

So they were having a full house for Thanksgiving. Anika grinned. Money was tight, sometimes, but you'd never know it by the looks of this table of delicious smelling food. Tonight wasn't about money; it was about seeing special guests sharing this meal. Aunt Viola entered the dining room, ready to light the candles. The doorbell rang and Marquetta ran to greet their guests. This was going to be a fantastic Thanksgiving.

APPLICATION

During this period of financial uncertainty, occasions such as Thanksgiving can become a reason for downsizing. However, let's stay focused on Christlike behavior. We show gratitude for the abundance of Christ's love; in doing so, we extend our generosity—with a meal and an opportunity to forego loneliness. Let's enjoy the bounteous pleasure of one another's company as we thank God for today, tomorrow, and eternity.

Be conscious of your thoughts and words today. Each time you find your attention drifting toward tomorrow's worries, force your mind back to the present day. Find at least one pleasant thing to say about the present moment. Thank the Lord!

PRAYER

Lord, help us to keep our thoughts and words where they belong. Teach us to have thankful minds, hearts, and spirits that are grounded in our trust that You already have tomorrow under control. Amen.

YOU ARE MY PILLAR...

*"And the Lord went before them by day in a pillar of a cloud,
to lead them the way; and by night in a pillar of fire,
to give them light; to go by day and night."*

Exodus 13:21

Viola Sutter lit the candles and checked the table. Anika did a good job of putting the food on the table. Marquetta helped with the cooking. Now the girls were being hostesses, showing that they were glad to have guests in their home.

She began pouring ice water into the glasses. Mr. Forrest entered the dining room and asked if she needed any help. She told him to let her and her nieces serve him. "It's a fine family you've got," he said.

"It sure is something to be thankful for," she agreed. As she took the pitcher back to the kitchen, she remembered a Thanksgiving when the girls' mother had passed away two months before. Marquetta was eight and Anika was four. Viola had quite a time of it, but she was determined to be the parent she knew her sister had been. When Thanksgiving came, Viola and the girls spent the day serving meals at a homeless shelter.

That was 10 years ago; every Thanksgiving since was an occasion for generosity. Anika held out her hand to her aunt; she joined the circle of prayer that Marquetta was starting. Her girls were leading the way.

APPLICATION

God should always be at the forefront of our thoughts and behavior. While we are thankful for opportunities to entertain people we care about, our deepest gratitude belongs to God. This was the case when God walked with the Children of Israel, going before them with a pillar of a cloud during daytime and lighting the way at night with a pillar of fire.

Today, reflect on some of the special occasions you've experienced or planned. Thank God for being with you—even when you got caught up in the planning and the day itself and sometimes forgot about His presence. Share at least one of your memories with a friend or family member, including moments that made you truly thankful for the experience. Then listen as the other person shares as well. Make such sharing a regular part of family gatherings.

PRAYER

Lord, help us to rejoice at all times. We thank You for the sweetness of Your presence during our darkest hours. Thank You for memories that give us hope and abiding joy. Amen.

DAY 3 / THANK YOU FOR MY ENEMIES!
THEY MAY SPEAK THE TRUTH...

*"But love ye your enemies, and do good, and lend,
hoping for nothing again; and your reward shall be great,
and ye shall be the children of the Highest."*
Luke 6:35a

James washed the dishes while his sister Gwen dried them. Conversation, laughter, and music from the living room provided background for the running water and clatter of dishes. Gwen studied her brother's profile. He seemed calmer.

After she asked him about his mood, James shrugged. "I've been thanking God for my enemies—or at least one enemy." He washed a plate and held it under the faucet. "Remember me telling you about that guy at work and the arguments we've had?" Gwen nodded. "Well, a few weeks ago, he told me that I was too argumentative, I made things unpleasant at work, and I wouldn't listen to constructive criticism."

James grinned. "I was about to open my mouth to give him a piece of my mind, when something clicked. I pictured people I loved trying to talk to me—and I could see myself arguing back. I finally got the message." He shook his head and smiled. "It took my enemy to teach me the truth. I've been thanking God for him ever since."

APPLICATION

Why should we love our enemies? As believers, we are commissioned to spread the Good News of God's love, His mercy, His forgiveness, and His covenant of reconciliation to all people (Acts 1:8). Jesus demonstrated this in His encounter with the woman at the well and in the parable of the good Samaritan (Luke 10:25-37; John 4:4-42). Why does the Lord allow enemies? Loved ones are committed to us. Sometimes they don't tell us what we really need to hear. Our enemies don't care about our feelings; when we will not listen to those we love, God allows our enemies to show us our weaknesses and flaws.

Today, think about a confrontation that you have had with an enemy. Put your hand over your heart and calm down, sister. Ask the Lord to reveal truth to you, to show you some treasure that your enemy might have unexpectedly brought to you. With a thankful spirit, meditate on what you learn and then pray.

PRAYER

Lord, help us to love our enemies so that we might extend Your grace to them. Lord, help us to hear the words of truth that come from the mouths of our enemies. Lord, teach us to love as You do. Amen.

EVEN IN-LAWS AND OTHER IRRITATING PEOPLE...

"And it came to pass, as Jesus sat at meat in the house, behold, many publicans and sinners came and sat down with him and his disciples. And when the Pharisees saw it, they said unto his disciples, Why eateth your Master with publicans and sinners? But when Jesus heard that, he said unto them, They that be whole need not a physician, but they that are sick."

Matthew 9:10-12

Alena smiled at her husband, James and watched him doting on his mother. Alena was really glad to be here at Mother Betty's house. Long ago, at Betty's insistence she dropped the use of "in-law." Mother Betty welcomed her and loved her, more than Alena had ever hoped would happen. It was a blessing to be part of such a loving and generous family; it made her feel whole and wanted.

Mother Betty treated everyone this way. There was always enough food for anyone who stopped by, always a chair for anyone who wanted to stick around a while. Every person was welcome, no matter how unwelcome they might be elsewhere. Mother Betty made room.

APPLICATION

Most of us have no trouble welcoming those without flaws or blemishes—those who cause us no grief. We're thankful and happy to welcome those who bring us joy and cheer. But we'd rather not include "strangers" with unfamiliar habits—and sometimes that can mean in-laws. Perhaps we should remind ourselves of the Lord's example and share ourselves with those who often feel unwanted or work our nerves.

During this holiday season, let's take a lesson from Mother Betty. Think of one person who would benefit from your love today. Pray about him or her. Ask the Lord what you could do to be a blessing to that person and do it today.

PRAYER

Lord, help us to be thankful for and love all people, especially those who challenge us. Amen.

IT MUST BE DEACON MURRAY...

"And it came to pass, that, as I made my journey,
and was come nigh unto Damascus about noon,
suddenly there shone from heaven a great light round about me."

Acts 22:6

Mother Betty peered around the corner at her son James and her granddaughter Geneva. "What are the two of you cutting up about?"

Geneva laughed. "Oh, Grandma, we were just praying for you, using the prayer of Jabez. Everybody is praying it these days—you know, expand your territory and all that."

Geneva's father James nodded. "We were saying that you make every day special for everyone you come in contact with. We were talking about what we could pray for you to have. Maybe a new car—"

"Or a new house!" Geneva inserted. "But it looks as if you have everything you want."

Mother Betty nodded. "Yes, there isn't anything more that I could want."

"So, we decided," Geneva pointed at herself and her dad, "that we'll just leave it to God. We'll let Him surprise us."

The doorbell rang, and Alena walked into the living room escorting Deacon Murray, a widower in the church who was bearing flowers. "I hope it isn't too late to call," he said.

"Something came over me suddenly and I felt like coming here."

Betty looked from Deacon Murray to Geneva. "Well," she said and cleared her throat.

"This isn't bad timing, is it?" Deacon Murray asked.

Betty smiled. "No. Unexpected, but I wouldn't say it was bad." She winked at her granddaughter and son.

APPLICATION

We pray for God to bless us, to expand our territory, to make us over; but we rarely leave room for Him to surprise us. We look for a sign or a plan that will tell us where things are headed. Like Saul traveling down the Damascus Road, we are pretty sure of what's ahead. But sometimes what we need is an unexpected change of course.

Think of one person who you would love to have a sudden blessing. Ask the Lord to bless the person suddenly, however the Lord sees fit. Then, ask the Lord to bless you in the way that most delights Him.

PRAYER

Lord, we love You, and we will wait for Your sudden appearance because we understand that "sudden" is within Your power. Amen.

WEEK ONE: DREAMS

DAY 1 / DREAMS: FANTASY OR REALITY?

A DREAM COME TRUE...

"In a dream, in a vision of the night, when deep sleep falleth upon men, in slumberings upon the bed; Then he openeth the ears of men, and sealeth their instruction."

Job 33:15-16

A close friend called to tell me about a dream she had. She saw herself in another city surrounded by children, to whom she was giving instruction.

Months later, she called me from New York. One of the world's largest nonprofit agencies—Children's Research and Development—had flown her in to interview for the position of vice president. They offered her the job and she accepted, fulfilling a goal to have a job helping children.

APPLICATION

Since God is omnipresent, it is possible for Him to speak to us while we sleep—instructing us or warning us, preparing us or repairing us. We may dismiss our dreams, thinking they are mere fanciful notions or the result of eating too late. As women of God, we cannot afford to dismiss them completely. We must be alert to hear God. Trust God with your dreams—the daydreams, the goals, and the dreams you have while asleep.

Keep a dream journal: Record the dreams you have while sleeping by writing down whatever you remember as soon as you awaken. Also write down the dreams you have for your life. Pray and ask God to make you open to what He says to you.

PRAYER

Father God, from this day forth, please give me the insight and wisdom to seek to understand what You are saying to me. Give me discernment and wisdom, Lord. I thank You and I praise You. In Jesus' holy name. Amen.

DAY 2: / WHEN THEY'RE TOO GOOD TO BE TRUE

A MOUTH FILLED WITH LAUGHTER...

"When the Lord turned again the captivity of Zion, we were like them that dream. Then was our mouth filled with laughter, and our tongue with singing: then said they among the heathen, The Lord hath done great things for them."

Psalm 126:1-2

Before Steve met Gina, he lived the life of a promiscuous bachelor. Then he turned to God, began to attend church, and met Gina. However, Steve became bored and gradually regressed to his bachelor behavior. Their marriage ended; Gina was devastated. She became a recluse, gained weight, and was depressed.

She began to have the same dream over and over of being in a happy relationship. A friend sent her a satin ring pillow for her birthday, saying that she saw Gina getting remarried. For three years, these dreams continued; but Gina thought they were too good to be true.

When she went on a trip abroad, Gina met a man of God. Soon afterward, they were married. Now, 12 years later, she is still happily married—with three children and a life full of the glory of God.

APPLICATION

Life can be challenging; it can be frustrating when troubles arise or an achievement seems beyond our reach. God wants to teach us that it is by His grace that we live, and not by our good works. Like the people in Psalm 126, we dream of a bright future when our mouths will be filled with laughter as we sing praises to the Lord. If we will be patient and trust Him, God will turn our lives around.

Ask yourself what you have desired for a long time. On small pieces of paper, write down brief summaries of this powerful desire and slip the pieces of paper into various places. As you come across the summary, pause and pray about it as you remind yourself of your dream. Have faith in God and be patient.

PRAYER

Dear Lord, please give me the heart to praise You for what You are doing in my life. Help me to run this race with patience and accept Your gifts of grace. Amen.

DAY 3 / THE HEART OF THE DREAMER
AN UNDERSTANDING HEART...

"In Gibeon the Lord appeared to Solomon in a dream by night: and God said, Ask what I shall give thee. And Solomon said,...Give therefore thy servant an understanding heart to judge thy people, that I may discern between good and bad."

1 Kings 3:5-6a, 9a

When I accepted Jesus as my Lord and Savior at the age of 24, I asked the Lord to give me wisdom and discernment. At the time, I deeply wanted a husband and children; but my request was for discernment and wisdom.

Over the years, I did marry and have two kids. I've been through more struggles in my personal life and my career than I ever imagined could happen to me. But my faith has remained strong. As it turns out, when I look back over the past several years, my request when I was 24 was the best I could have asked God to provide. God knows the desire of our hearts. He knew that what I really desired was wisdom and discernment.

APPLICATION

King Solomon asked God for a discerning heart to judge his people and be able to distinguish between right and wrong. Because Solomon was humble, his heart was pure, and his dreams for his people were what God desired, God told him that He would give him riches and honor, as well as a wise and understanding heart. What a gracious God we serve! Imagine what God will do for us, without our asking, if our hearts are turned toward Him.

Search your heart each day to see if there is anything that will keep you from hearing God clearly. Then remember Paul's words, found in Philippians 4:8, about what we should fill our minds with. Ask God to help you fill your mind with those things.

PRAYER

I ask You, Lord God, to purify my heart daily. I understand that in order to conceive of an idea and bring it into practice I must let You guide me. I pray for Your guidance and Your wisdom. Amen.

DAY 4 / THE DREAM HATERS
REJOICE IN A DREAM FULFILLED...

"And Joseph dreamed a dream, and he told it his brethren: and they hated him yet the more. And when they saw him afar off, even before he came near unto them, they conspired against him to slay him."
Genesis 37:5, 18

Nikki, Cindy, and Tina were close friends. They attended the same high school and college, and all of them majored in broadcast communications. After graduation, they moved to Hollywood to pursue their careers. Then they began making different choices.

While Tina and Nikki drifted and often took disreputable jobs, Cindy worked for a company owned by Christians. Though the company was small, she supervised some successful projects. Within a year, Cindy met and grew close to Bob, a nice, Christian man. Because it was looking like marriage, she wanted Tina and Nikki to meet him. She hadn't spoken to them in a long time and thought this was a good opportunity to catch up while introducing Bob.

During dinner Nikki and Tina talked about their wild adolescence. Since she'd given up those habits right after she relocated to California, Cindy was uncomfortable; she could tell that Bob felt the same way. Her friends ignored Cindy and Bob as they spoke about hanging out together, getting high, and being promiscuous. Then Tina said, "Cindy, do you think you can still have babies after your three surgeries?"

Bob asked, "What surgeries, sweetie? Are you all right?"

"Yes, honey, it's nothing," Cindy answered, blushing. "It was a long time ago. My body has since healed, and I've gotten to know God. I'll give you the details later."

APPLICATION

What causes friends to say things that may destroy lives? Cindy's friends hated to see her dreams coming true: She had a satisfying job at a reputable company and was about to marry a Christian. In Genesis 37, we read about Joseph and his brothers, who were threatened by the dreams God gave him about his future. They sold him into slavery. Nevertheless, his dreams came to pass. We don't have to be afraid of someone else's dreams and other people's contentment and prosperity. These events are in God's hands. God has created all of us in His image to fulfill His purpose and destiny.

Have an honest self-assessment. When might you have said something regrettable in response to a friend, neighbor, or family member announcing an achievement accomplished or a dream they are striving to fulfill? Ask God to help you reassess how you can respond helpfully and with spirited encouragement to dreams that you and your loved ones have for themselves and their families.

PRAYER

Father, I want to bless the dreams and visions You give to me and to others. Father, I bless my friends' dreams, and I desire to be a support to them. Amen.

DAY 5 / SISTERS NEEDED TO INTERPRET
GIVE GOD THE GLORY...

"And they said unto him, We have dreamed a dream, and there is no interpreter of it. And Joseph said unto them, Do not interpretations belong to God? tell me them, I pray you."

Genesis 40:8

Lana was a young woman of 17 whose family lived next door to my brother and sister-in-law. One day, my sister-in-law Phyllis told me that after Lisa had been at a sleepover at Lana's, she told Phyllis that the girls called the Psychic Network to get a reading done.

Phyllis said that she thought it was "kind of cool" that the girls could do this. I tactfully told her what the Bible says about divination.

She asked, "Beatrice, what are we supposed to do when we are confused about something and seeking an answer? Psychics can give us some answers."

My heart sank. I told Phyllis not to take my word for it. She should read Genesis 29 to 31, Genesis 40 to 41, and Exodus 7. I urged her to pray to God for direction.

APPLICATION

As Beatrice pointed out, there are a number of Scriptures that will inform us about dreams and appropriate interpreters of dreams. In Genesis 29—31, we read about dreams from the story of Jacob and Laban. In Genesis 40—41, dreams were part of God's help with

Joseph's developing wisdom. We need to use our relationships to help others interpret God's Word. During this time of uncertainty, many people are turning to psychics and similarly fraudulent resources because of a mistaken belief that they know about the future. When someone mentions curiosity about psychics, make sure you have scriptural evidence that can help their learning process.

PRAYER

Our Father, we come before You this day knowing that You are the solution to what many call a chaotic, dying world. Lord, we thank You for the Word and the privilege and opportunity to serve You in this great hour when so many are seeking answers. Amen.

DECEMBER

WEEK TWO: COMMUNICATION

DAY 1 / IN THE MIDST OF IT ALL

MEDITATION IS A QUIET CONVERSATION WITH YOUR SOUL...

*"Give ear to my words, O Lord, consider my meditation. Lead me,
O Lord, in thy righteousness because of mine enemies;
make thy way straight before my face."*

Psalm 5:1, 8

Jocelyn had decided to give meditation a try. She had some ideas in the back of her mind and thought that meditation would help them emerge. However, the idea of meditation was easier than the practice. In the background was the noise of the TV in the family room downstairs. Then there was her son's video game in a nearby room. And no matter how she tried to concentrate, she heard her daughter's laughter, probably from a cell phone conversation, and her seven-year-old twins were playing in the backyard.

She opened the bedroom door and shouted at her kids to be quiet. Then she shut the door and returned to her meditation. But more thoughts disrupted her. She needed to call the plumber, her husband Mike was due home soon from grocery shopping, and her stomach growled, reminding her about lunchtime. With so many noises and so many details in her mind, she wondered how any woman succeeded at meditation.

APPLICATION

Meditation can help you understand an issue and seek a resolution. When you quiet your mind of internal chatter and distractions, you enable your thoughts and feelings to attain calm and peacefulness which then can open communication with God. Despite the challenge of achieving a quiet location, meditation is not a luxury. This essential tool allows you to understand your place in the world. When you meditate, as we read about David doing in Psalm 5, you come to a greater understanding of your situation as you seek God's help with the best solution.

Find a safe, private place today that you can use for meditation. If you are meditating at home, let family members know that you require a few private, quiet minutes on a regular basis. Try to eliminate outside stimulus and be still as you commune with God. After a few meditative experiences, notice your attitude toward daily life and the quality of your prayers.

PRAYER

Lord, I humbly ask that You help me be as placid as the waters You calmed. Please continue to guide me toward the path You intend. Please grant me peace of mind so that I may see the opportunities You present to me even when they seem to be more about tribulation than triumph. Amen.

DAY 2 / PROVIDENCE AND PRAYER
PRETTY PLEASE...

*"The eyes of all wait upon thee; and thou givest them their meat
in due season. Thou openest thine hand, and satisfiest the desire
of every living thing."*
Psalm 145:15-16

When Thelma entered the kitchen, she saw that her sons Bertrand and Baraka were at it again. Bertrand had decided to use lunchtime to teach Baraka lessons in manners. Of course, this made Baraka unhappy. She sat down between them and asked for an explanation.

Bertrand said, "Baraka snatched the mustard away from me even though I told him to wait his turn."

"Mama, he wouldn't give the mustard to me. He wanted me to ask right, to say please or something."

"That's what you're supposed to do," Bertrand said.

"Well, yeah. But why do I have to wait until he's ready to give me what I want?"

Thelma sighed. She really wanted her sons to get along with each other, and she also appreciated Bertrand's efforts at teaching his younger brother. Before saying anything, she prayed for God's mediating help.

APPLICATION

God wants us to speak to Him and one another properly. Do you feel that fulfilling communication seems like a nearly unachievable goal? God has a plan for you—trust Him to communicate about it as you learn lessons along every step of the journey. Today, tell God plainly what you need, and be patient as you grow in your ability to understand His response. Consider what you want and be clear. When you communicate with clarity, you take a step closer to God.

PRAYER

Dear Lord, You challenge me to be the best I can be, and I value each lesson. Please let me see the path I should choose. Thank You for the light that You provide. I love You, Lord. Amen.

DAY 3 / KNOWLEDGE OF SOUL, MIND, AND BODY
DO I LOOK FAT?

"I will praise thee; for I am fearfully and wonderfully made: marvellous are thy works; and that my soul knoweth right well."

Psalm 139:14

Felicity and Sherice were celebrating Sherice's birthday at their favorite restaurant. Sherice said, "You're practically drooling, Felicity. Why don't you order the chocolate cheesecake you're staring at in the bakery case?"

"I really shouldn't. I am trying to lose weight, you know. I thought you were supposed to encourage me."

Sherice laughed. "I am encouraging you...to get the cheesecake! C'mon, we can split it. Want to get ice cream, too? It's my birthday. It's not like we eat like this every day, right?"

APPLICATION

Communication includes our bodies—how we talk about them, what they communicate about us, and the messages we need to reconsider sending and receiving. When our selections of food and drink are nourishing and come from healthy sources, these choices build up our strength. For those of us feeding family members, our choices can reinforce family members' health as well. The body is the Holy Spirit's temple; we are "fearfully and wonderfully made," and what we eat and drink can show we know that God loves us.

Be mindful of what you put in your mouth today. Choose a varied diet, rich in fruit, vegetables, protein, whole grains, and low-fat dairy. Don't overindulge; occasionally sweeten your plate. Exercise regularly to strengthen your body. See your physician regularly to check for problems before they become untreatable. Remember that God created your body and it is His temple—let your body speak of healthy goodness.

PRAYER

O Lord, help me to make reasonable portions of healthful food and drink that respect my body. Help me exercise so that my bones are strong. Remind me to go to the doctor before I need to. Lord, I want my body to communicate my love for You. Amen.

CAN BARELY HEAR MYSELF THINK ABOVE ALL THE CLUCKING!

"A divine sentence is in the lips of the king: his mouth transgresseth not in judgment. Pleasant words are as a honeycomb, sweet to the soul, and health to the bones. An ungodly man diggeth up evil: and in his lips there is as a burning fire."

Proverbs 16:10, 24, 27

Three women sat in the lobby of a movie theatre, offering comments about people who walked by. "I can just tell she must be easy," one of the threesome said to the others. "That short dress, the way she walks—she definitely looks like a loose woman."

The others nodded, and then one of them half-covered her mouth. "That woman moved into my apartment complex a month ago. One of my neighbors told me that woman keeps a messy house."

The third woman nodded in the direction of a pair of shoes that a passerby was wearing. "Now those shoes are definitely ugly!"

Sitting across from them, a woman was waiting for her date to join her. The tone of the threesome reminded her of a gaggle of geese: honk, honk, honk!

APPLICATION

How many times have you witnessed or participated in dialogue like this? Mean-spirited chatter is a waste of time, sisters. It's nice to laugh, have fun, and learn about each other. It is another thing entirely to engage in spitefulness, to spread rumors, or circulate sad truths. People are imperfect and need understanding from one another. None of us knows the intentions of another person's heart, but we all need compassion and forgiveness.

Decide that unless you can speak kindly of someone, you won't speak about the person at all. When you're around people who begin to gossip, don't stand quietly by, absorbing the negative energy. If you are unable to challenge the gossipers to lift the tone of their conversation, remove yourself. Or share a positive experience you have had. It will soon be apparent that when it comes to juicy gossip and careless whispers, you're just not that kind of woman.

PRAYER

Lord, help me to not sit in judgment of others or stand idly by while folks talk poorly about one another. Keep my heart pure and my words kind. O Lord, please keep me always mindful of Your will and my ability to communicate with You in mind. Amen.

DAY 5 / WHAT THE WORLD NEEDS

DEEPER THAN OOH, BABY, BABY...

"As the Father hath loved me, so have I loved you: continue ye in my love.
This is my commandment, That ye love one another, as I have loved you."
John 15:9, 12

She was crying when I came upon her. She sat against the wall next to a small cart loaded with bags. I had no idea how far she had come, but her tears moved me. She whispered in synch with each teardrop: "I need to go home. Please can someone give me some money so I can get home? I just want to get home. Please can...."

I gave her all the money I had. It wasn't much, but even pennies are precious. She quietly thanked me, got up slowly, and pushed her cart toward a bus stop. Since I gave her my cash and I was on a strict budget, my dinner plans had suddenly changed. I headed home, thanking God that I am my sisters' keeper.

APPLICATION

Putting kindness first is a challenge; but we must keep our eyes and ears open, ready to hear what's being asked of us. Most of us are experiencing lean times, but others are experiencing even tougher times and desperately need help. Being aware of everyone around us, witnessing their trials and offering help and a kind word lets them know that, praise God, no one walks alone.

Find a way to improve the quality of life for the poor in your community. Take your children with you and teach them to do the same. One person at a time, we can make a difference—and Christians should lead the charge so we communicate to the world that we are obeying God's golden rule.

PRAYER

Lord, help me to see beyond myself so that I may help others. Please open my ears and my heart to the needs of my community. Let me be as considerate of my neighbor as I would hope she would be of me. Do not let me pass someone who has fallen without pausing to help them rise. Please, help me to remember I can make a difference. Amen.

DECEMBER

WEEK THREE: PREGNANCY

DAY 1 / CONCEIVING THE DREAM

I WANT IT SO BAD, I CAN ALMOST TASTE IT...

"But as it is written, Eye hath not seen, nor ear heard, neither have entered into the heart of man, the things which God hath prepared for them that love him."

1 Corinthians 2:9

Since the age of nine, Lydia had known she wanted to be a doctor. She enjoyed visits with her pediatrician, Dr. Baker. The doctor had a soft, gentle nature, a sincere smile, and a willingness to answer Lydia's questions.

Lydia enthusiastically watched medical shows on television—dramas and documentaries. The thought of saving lives intrigued Lydia. She knew what she wanted—and she wanted it so bad, she could almost taste it. To Lydia, the idea of becoming a doctor seemed like the best thing she could do with her life.

APPLICATION

God created everything with and for a purpose (Jeremiah 1:5). Before any of us were conceived, He knew us. He made each one of us as special and unique individuals. Just as a woman's desire to have a child often leads to conception, our strong desire to fulfill our purpose in life begins when our minds conceive it. So it is with the desires of our hearts and our dreams for the future. We anticipate their fulfillment, we step out in faith, we do all we can, and we trust.

Write the sentences below on small pieces of paper and place them on your mirrors, the refrigerator, your personal planner, car dashboard, and every other place you know you will see them:

* I am fearfully and wonderfully made (Psalm 139:14).

* As I delight myself in the Lord, He will give me the desires of my heart (Psalm 37:4).

* The Lord is close to the brokenhearted and saves those who are crushed in spirit (Psalm 34:18).

As you go about your daily tasks, these statements of belief will remind you constantly of God's goodness.

PRAYER

Heavenly Father, thank You for creating me with a purpose and the desire to fulfill that purpose. I surrender myself to You. Lord, You know the desires of my heart and will enable me to see them come true in my life. I give all glory to You. In Jesus' name. Amen.

DAY 2 / BE PREPARED!

I NEED TO GET MY HAIR AND NAILS DONE!

"So Jotham became mighty, because he prepared his ways before the Lord his God."

2 Chronicles 27:6

Saturday night was the long-awaited event of the year. While shopping for a dress to wear, she saw one of her sorority sisters.

"Are you going to the gala on Saturday?" Mina asked.

"I sure am," said Riane. "There's going to be so many professionals there. I'm hoping to network and meet people who may be able to help me with my career. I need to get my hair and nails done!"

Mina nodded and agreed it was a good idea to show people you at your best. "Something else is good to do. When I was job hunting, I stayed on my knees. I asked God to lead me in the right direction and prepare me for anything I have to face," Mina said with an encouraging smile.

"Oh, believe me, I will be prepared." Riane pointed out that she'd gotten business cards printed so she could distribute her contact information, and she'd revised her resumé to include volunteer work at a neighborhood library and her church's Bible camp.

157

"Those are great ideas," Mina told her and added, "The Bible also says that we have to be prepared for Jesus when He returns because we don't know when that will be. I believe it's in Matthew 24:44: 'Therefore be ye also ready: for in such an hour as ye think not the Son of man cometh.'"

APPLICATION

We know that God is preparing for our arrival. Jesus said, "I go to prepare a place for you" (John 14:2b). We know, too, that while we are here on earth, He is preparing us for whatever we will give birth to in our lives. Stay in touch with God and trust Him. Study your Bible. Go to church and listen carefully. Ask the Lord to show you how to seek His face. Ask yourself if your life contains unnecessary or harmful habits. Get rid of the clutter and focus on preparing your body, mind, and spirit for what God has in store for you.

PRAYER

Father, thank You for Your love, grace, and mercy. Lord, prepare me for the things You have in store for me. I trust You with my future. Thank You always. In Jesus' name. Amen.

DAY 3 / THE BITTER AND THE SWEET
IS ALL THIS REALLY NECESSARY?

"But rejoice, inasmuch as ye are partakers of Christ's sufferings; that,
when his glory shall be revealed, ye may be glad also with exceeding joy."
1 Peter 4:13

Karrah rarely slept well. Her schedule was too full. She had a hectic routine, but in just a few months she could graduate with a psychology degree. After that, her goal was to spend more time in her career and less time on some of the tasks that crowded her schedule now. As a single mother of three children working two jobs, the process was painful. Her feet and back hurt from the hours spent standing at one of her jobs; she was developing arthritis, and lack of sleep caused migraines.

"Is all the pain and suffering necessary?" her mother asked. She wondered aloud if her daughter should postpone her career plans.

"Well, Mom," Karrah began, "I think about our forefathers and the suffering they endured for our freedom. Then there are athletes who rigorously train to perform at peak capacity. Most importantly, I think about Jesus and the suffering He endured to save us from our sins. I'm prepared to suffer a little now because of the joy I will experience."

APPLICATION

Jesus looked on His suffering as an opportunity to rejoice—not in the suffering but in the outcome (Hebrews 2:9-10). We may get weary as we strive to reach our goals, but we are encouraged to continue so that we can rejoice (Galatians 6:9).

Concentrate on a difficult time in your past. How did God ultimately bring you out of it? If the difficulty is happening now, what gives you confidence that your outcome will be worthwhile? Remind yourself that God comes through for you always.

PRAYER

Father, I give You honor and praise. Help me not to tire and turn away from the efforts I make to achieve something great. I know You are the ultimate reward. In Jesus' name. Amen.

DAY 4 / THE DANGEROUS D's: DOUBT, DISCOURAGEMENT, AND DISPIRITEDNESS
TOO HOT TO HANDLE?

"For verily I say unto you, That whosoever shall say unto this mountain, Be thou removed, and be thou cast into the sea; and shall not doubt in his heart, but shall believe that those things which he saith shall come to pass; he shall have whatsoever he saith."

Mark 11:23

For years, April had prayed about her employment situation, rarely experiencing satisfaction. She loved the pay at her current job, but the work was wearing her down.

April accepted her current job as a blessing from the Lord. At first she arrived early, stayed late, and volunteered to take on more responsibility. But she soon realized that her hard work was problematic. Her boys were already asleep by the time she got home—and she was sleeping very little.

However, her options seemed limited. If she quit her job, her family would suffer financially, the career she had worked so hard for would suffer, and she might not get another job that paid as well. Her husband supported her staying in her job because he enjoyed all the things her money helped them buy. But she was unhappy and feeling overwhelmed. The situation was "too hot to handle."

APPLICATION

Does that situation sound familiar? Did you think a situation was God's will but then realized that it may have been God teaching you a lesson? When you have a big decision to make, the enemy will play on worries and concerns, making you fearful. Satan creates doubt, discouragement, and dispiritedness. Satan wants to steal our hopes, kill our dreams, and destroy our confidence in God (John 10:10). But Satan is no match for God. He is already defeated. So our focus should not be on him and his lies, but on God and His love for us.

Whenever you are discouraged, dispirited, or begin to doubt God, remind yourself that you are His child (Matthew 13:38). Diligently follow Him, and you will find that He is generous and gracious and always answers prayer. Compile a series of Scriptures that offer the opposite of the three D's—that focus on encouragement, uplifting of the spirit, and confidence. Embed the Scriptures you have chosen within yourself by studying them over and over. Notice that the influence of the "dangerous D's" is fading from your mind.

PRAYER

Father, thank You for choosing me. Please help me to stand on Your promises, not wavering or doubting. I give You praise always. Amen.

DAY 5 / AFTER PREPARATION, RESULTS!
BRING IT ON...

"And whatsoever we ask, we receive of him, because we keep his commandments, and do those things that are pleasing in his sight."
1 John 3:22

Bethany's heart pounded as her car inched closer to the hotel. After 10 years of hard work and diligent fasting and praying, she was on her way to her film's premiere in Manhattan. Still, she wasn't sure how the movie would be received.

She was fully aware that the film industry did not receive African American filmmakers with open arms. After completing school, Bethany moved from Indiana to New York City, working odd jobs to pay bills. By obtaining the funding and with support from her peers, she completed her film. The words of Jeremiah 29 kept her going.

Bethany had kept her focus on the Lord and on her goal. God had been there for her every step of the way. Tonight was her big night. Even though she was afraid of what would happen next, she praised God for getting her to this point.

APPLICATION

Although Bethany was finally realizing her dream, she was afraid about its outcome. Generally, we women find it hard to recognize and accept God's blessings. We should be able to welcome God's desire to do good things for us. We should be just as eager to receive blessings for our hard work and dedication.

As a daughter of the King, stand boldly before the throne of grace and mercy. Offer up praise for the blessings God has given you. Read what the Bible says about blessings and reflect on the passages. Think about the idea of blessings throughout the day as you pray about the Scriptures you have read.

PRAYER

Father, help me to recognize that I am truly Your child. Help me to humbly accept Your good gifts and proclaim Your mighty name. I give You praise, Lord. Amen.

DECEMBER

WEEK FOUR: CHRISTMAS

DAY 1 / HOPE

MAKING A WAY OUT OF NO WAY...

"The people that walked in darkness have seen a great light."
Isaiah 9:2a

Tonya hung up the telephone, devastated. Since her husband's death five years earlier, she struggled to raise her son and daughter in a way that pleased God. Her job allowed her to be there when her children got home from school. She was active in her church and had her children participate in Sunday school and youth group activities. She monitored their homework. But lately things were going badly.

Her daughter's high school counselor told her that her daughter was a truant from school and was caught smoking marijuana. Tonya sank into a chair and sobbed. She had not felt as much sorrow since her husband's death. But then she remembered something comforting: Her husband was resting in the bosom of the Lord.

Tonya stopped crying. "I will not be defeated," she told herself, "because my hope is in the Lord." She knelt where she was and prayed for hope and strength. She stood up; the heaviness was gone and her spirit was lifted. The light of God was shining around her.

She called the school and made an appointment to see the counselor. By the power of God, she had the strength to help her daughter.

APPLICATION

Too often, when life burdens us, we wrestle using only our own strength and defeat rules us. But God's hope does not let us wallow in darkness, for His light leads us every step of the way. He wants us to walk through the world letting His light shine all around us (John 8:12). The Spirit of Christ is in us, and His light leads us from despair to hope, and then to victory.

Whenever you feel burdened, remember there is hope in the light of Jesus, which dwells in you. Let the strength of His light lead you away from your troubles and allow you to tear down every barrier that stands in your way. Share this message with others who have cumbersome loads in their lives and pray with them.

PRAYER

Dear Jesus, You are the light of the world. Your light casts out darkness and gives us the strength to hope when others see no hope. Help us to use that light. And then please, dear God, let others see that our hope comes from Your light within us. Amen.

SOMEONE YOU CAN COUNT ON...

"For unto us a child is born, unto us a son is given: and the government shall be upon his shoulder: and his name shall be called Wonderful, Counsellor, The mighty God, The everlasting Father, The Prince of Peace."
Isaiah 9:6

Tiffany picked at her salad as she waited for Barbara. She was thinking about making a career move and wanted to talk it over with Barbara. They planned to meet for lunch at noon. Tiffany arrived early enough to get their favorite corner booth. Each time she heard the chime of the bell that announced another customer's arrival, Tiffany looked toward the front of the restaurant. By 12:30, Tiffany ordered a garden salad, realizing that Barbara would arrive very late—if at all.

This had become Barbara's pattern. Whenever Tiffany needed to talk to her, Barbara was never there. They'd make plans to meet. But then Barbara stood her up.

Tiffany anxiously glanced at her watch, glanced at the entrance one more time, and realized she had to get back to work. "How could she do this to me, again?" she asked out loud. She pushed aside the plate of salad and signaled for her check so she could leave. She wondered if she'd ever again be able to count on the woman she thought was her best friend.

APPLICATION

We are all too willing to believe that another person can do what only God can do. When we do that, we set ourselves up for disappointment. We can count on God. Look at Isaiah 9:6. Every part of this verse demonstrates that God's promises come true and His presence brings us the ultimate peace. When we're troubled or in the process of making a decision, we should take it to Him in prayer. We can always count on His unceasing support and guidance.

Next time you need to make a decision, let Jesus lead you. Then go ahead and tell your friends what God has shown you. Share the wisdom the Lord has given you. Give praise and glory to the Father.

PRAYER

Dear Lord, help us to remember that You and You alone always keep Your promises. Show us in Your mighty way so that we can always count on You. Amen.

DAY 3 / GOD WITH US

PART OF A TEAM...

"Behold, a virgin shall be with child,
and shall bring forth a son, and they shall call his name Emmanuel,
which being interpreted is, God with us."

Matthew 1:23

Alana and Charles walked along the sidewalk. They usually walked after dinner on Sundays. They had done so since they were first married. Today the temperature was quite cold, and Charles noticed that Alana was shivering. He tried to take her hand, but she pulled away. She hadn't meant to, but she hurt his feelings. She wanted to say something, but she didn't seem to have the words.

They had been married five years but were no longer close. Something had gone terribly wrong since those first passionate, loving months. They were together but were distant from each other. The winter's day seemed a reflection of their marital state. She was afraid for their marriage—so fearful that her thoughts had caused her to shiver. And she found no comfort in his hand reaching out to her.

APPLICATION

When we feel as if we are alone in this world, remember that the name of the Lord— Emmanuel—means "God with us." We are never alone. As Christians, we are part of a team, and Jesus is our teammate. We walk this path together; we share in fellowship together; we partner in prayer together. The Christian faith is not a lone search for God. It is a joyous union with God. God is with us. Hallelujah! First, though, we must acknowledge Him. If we feel lost or alone, we can go to Him in prayer. If we are struggling to keep our marriage intact, we should kneel, as a couple, and ask Him to dwell in the midst of our union.

If you feel that you are alone in a particular situation or relationship, call on Jesus right now. He will be with us, even to the end of the world (Matthew 28:20). Invite Him into your prayer circle. Invite Him into your marriage. Invite Him to walk with you as you navigate situations on the job. Invite Him to lead you in the devotional time you set aside each day. When we follow Him, we are capable of anything He deems us to achieve.

PRAYER

Thank You Lord, for being a living God, always present. Help us to remember to call upon You. Help us to remember to recognize You as You walk with us, talk to us, and dwell within us. Amen.

DAY 4 / NOT ABANDONED
THERE FOR THE LONG HAUL...

"For with God nothing shall be impossible."
Luke 1:37

Leah dreamed of opening a Christian bookstore that also hosted Bible studies and teen fellowship groups. She envisioned it as her business as well as her ministry. She had fervently sought the Lord's will and prayed about it daily. She'd begun saving seed money for the business and established a timetable for quitting her current job and devoting her energy to realizing her dream.

One day, Leah found the perfect location, an abandoned storefront with a "for lease" sign. It was in the middle of a commercial strip in the heart of town. She began making mental plans for its renovation. She was sure this was the building!

At home that evening, she called the number on the sign and asked to speak to the owner. He told her that an international corporation was planning to buy property in the area and construct a state-of-the-art factory. The property she was interested in was no longer available; he planned to sell it to the corporation for big money.

Leah felt lost and dejected. Now, she wasn't sure if her dream would ever come true.

APPLICATION

Even though we have sought the Lord's will, we may feel that our strongest dreams will always remain beyond our grasp. God knows how we feel. That's why He reminded us in Luke 1:37 that with God all things are possible. Consider how Mary probably felt when the angel Gabriel announced that she would conceive a child by the Holy Spirit. She was engaged to be married. Now her life would change forever. She had a good reputation but now ill repute would surround her. But the angel's message was that nothing is impossible with God. The Lord encouraged Mary, and He encourages us, to keep the faith and never lose hope. When we seek God's will, our dreams will be realized because He is with us for the long haul.

What dreams have you nurtured in your heart? Today, assure yourself that God is with you from the birth of your dreams to the reality of their unfolding. Thank God for the coming of His Son Jesus Christ. If we stand firm and seek His will, nothing—absolutely nothing—is impossible.

PRAYER

Dear God, my Lord and Savior, help me to always seek Your will in my life as I experience the process of bringing my efforts to fruition. Thank You for Your perfect will; with You, nothing is impossible.

DAY 5 / TIDINGS OF GREAT JOY
FEELING GOOD INSIDE...

"And Mary said, My soul doth magnify the Lord, And my spirit hath rejoiced in God my Saviour."

Luke 1:46-47

The kids were sound asleep in bed and her husband had fallen asleep on the living room sofa. Johnetta finished wrapping the last Christmas gift and put it neatly under the tree. She stood up, looking at the tree's twinkling lights and ornaments, and smiled. She thought about the reason behind all of the special music, cookie baking, and gift giving: We have a living God whose birth we celebrate at this time each year. There was nothing better than that.

Johnetta felt good inside. Her joy soared within her. She walked over to her husband on the sofa, bent down, and kissed him on the forehead. "Merry Christmas, honey," she whispered. "Merry Christmas!"

APPLICATION

We have a living God. That thought alone should fill us with unimaginable joy and thanksgiving. Our God walked on this earth, felt what we feel, and saw what we see. He understands us. Above all else, He loves us. That is why we celebrate His birth each Christmas season. No greater gift has ever been given to humanity than our Savior's gift, who freely offers us eternal life. It is no wonder that the Magi followed the star and worshiped Him (Matthew 2:1-2, 9-11). Let us rejoice in Jesus Christ our Savior!

During this season, spend some quiet moments reflecting on the grace of God. Jesus was born to save us from our sins. Express your joy to the world.

PRAYER

Lord Jesus, You have blessed us more than we will ever know. We thank You and rejoice in Your goodness and grace. Help us to count our blessings and feel good inside because You sent us Your Son, Jesus Christ, the living God. Amen.

WEEK ONE: POWER LIVING

DAY 1 / WHAT DO YOU SEE?

HELP! I JUST CAN'T SEE MY WAY OUT...

"And Elisha prayed, and said, Lord, I pray thee, open his eyes, that he may see. And the Lord opened the eyes of the young man; and he saw: and, behold, the mountain was full of horses and chariots of fire round about Elisha."

2 Kings 6:17

The phone rang. Shelia's heart pounded and her stomach knotted up, again. Checking caller ID, she saw it was the mortgage company calling again. She was three months behind on the mortgage, and the bank was set to begin foreclosure procedures if she didn't catch up in the next 10 days. Shelia's event planning business was failing due to the downturn in the economy. And now that her husband had lost his job, they couldn't make ends meet without his salary. Hopeless and helpless, she didn't see a way out. As she wiped the tears from her face, the phone rang again and her insides did their usual gymnastics. She let the call go to voice mail.

APPLICATION

When you feel as though the enemy is about to swoop in to destroy you, what do you see? Do you see God's provision, God's answer, or God's protection? When Elisha prayed for his servant's eyes to be opened, he prayed having already seen God's provision. Know that so, too, your answer, your provision, your protection is already surrounding you. God's hand is at work in your life. In order to live life as God intended, you must see yourself as God sees you—a winner! Begin to recognize the Lord's provisions, protection, and deliverance encamped around you so that you will be ready, willing, and able to defeat all the enemies that try to come against you!

PRAYER

Lord, open my eyes that I might see. Allow me to see Your provision for my life. I believe that You love me enough to deliver me from my enemies. I want to see my enemies defeated. Help me today and every day to walk by faith and not by sight. In Jesus' name. Amen.

DAY 2 / WHAT DO YOU HEAR?

LORD, SPEAK TO ME...

"And he said unto them, Take heed what ye hear: with what measure ye mete, it shall be measured to you: and unto you that hear shall more be given."

Mark 4:24

"Lord, I need your direction," whispered Joan. Sitting with her friend Susan, Joan shook her head slowly. "Sue, I need to know what to do. Do I quit my job to start this business, do I go back to school, or do I just let things be?"

"I don't have all the answers," Susan answered. "I know it can be difficult sometimes to hear what the Lord is saying, but I've found that the more I open myself up to hearing and receiving God's direction, the more He seems to speak to me."

"Really?" Joan replied.

"Yes, hearing from God can be difficult sometimes because we don't really know if we're hearing God. But the Bible talks about being doers of the Word and that only the doers get results!"

APPLICATION

How do we begin to become masters of hearing the voice of God? The process is simple. First, begin to develop a personal relationship with God. Begin to pour your heart and soul out to the Lord. Empty your mind of its cares and speak with God openly and honestly.

One way is to begin to journal. Write down all your cares and worries, and offer them up to the Lord. Open your spiritual ears to hear what our Father is saying.

Next, begin to focus on God. Begin to worship Him. Let Him know how important He is in your life, and ask Him to cleanse your heart and renew the spirit within. Tell Him how awesome He is—not for what He can do but for who He is!

Finally, be still, get quiet, and wait on God to answer. Continue to read God's Word and listen to the counsel of His people. God's answer will come. Remember, conversation is an exchange; and you have not had a conversation until God has responded!

PRAYER

Lord, I need to hear from You today and every day. I need You to show me what to do, how to live, where to go, and how to be the woman You want me to be. Lord, speak to me and I will follow. I receive Your direction, Your wisdom, and Your Word, and I will obey You. In Jesus' name. Amen.

DAY 3 / HOW SWEET DO YOU SMELL?
SETTING A FRAGRANT ATMOSPHERE IN OUR LIVES...

"Then took Mary a pound of ointment of spikenard, very costly, and anointed the feet of Jesus, and wiped his feet with her hair: and the house was filled with the odour of the ointment."
John 12:3

"I'm sorry baby, but your attitude stinks," Gladys scolded her daughter, Tasha. "And don't roll your eyes at me. Now please, go to your room!"

Tasha stormed off in a huff, and her mother continued the phone conversation her daughter had interrupted. "I'm sorry Janet, that girl is about to drive me crazy!"

"Calm down girl; she won't be a teenager forever," Janet laughed.

"I know, but her attitude stinks and it's affecting the whole household!"

"I understand. You remember when my daughter was Tasha's age; her attitude stank too," Janet said, laughing. "She's just experiencing growing pains. You need to get out the spiritual air freshener!"

"Spiritual air freshener?" Gladys chuckled. "What's that?"

179

"The Bible says that Mary took some very costly oil and anointed Jesus, and the sweet fragrance filled the house. It may seem strange, but you need to get some oil and begin to pray and anoint her and her room with it. And simply wait, God will turn her around!"

APPLICATION

When hell breaks loose at home—kids fighting, tempers flaring, attitudes out of control—call for peace in your home. Begin to rearrange the atmosphere and pour out your sacrifice to the Lord. Start by playing a praise and worship CD or singing a worship song to attract God's attention. Then, just as Mary took her best oil and anointed Jesus with it, begin to anoint your situation by giving God your best sacrifice of praise. As we begin to anoint Jesus with our worship, it will change the atmosphere and bring Jesus' sweet-smelling presence into our homes, hearts, and minds.

PRAYER

Lord, I want the atmosphere in and around my life to be so sweet-smelling that it is like the atmosphere in heaven! Today and every day, I promise to give You my worship, and I thank You for changing the atmosphere of my home and my life. In Jesus' name. Amen.

DAY 4 / ARE YOU FEELING MY PAIN, LORD?
I'M FALLING AND I CAN'T GET UP...

"For we have not an high priest which cannot be touched with the feeling of our infirmities; but was in all points tempted like as we are, yet without sin. Let us therefore come boldly unto the throne of grace, that we may obtain mercy, and find grace to help in time of need."

Hebrews 4:15-16

"Oh my, he's so fine! Jill told her friends, Mary and Sandy.

"Girl, don't you think you're moving a little too fast!" Sandy warned. "You just met the guy three weeks ago!"

"I know, but the way he makes me feel inside.... I think I'm falling for him," said Jill.

"Yeah, you're falling alright. I think he's got you all hot and bothered," Mary chimed in, laughing.

"Don't hate. Just because he's good looking, got bank, and treats me like a lady.... Besides, Jesus wouldn't send me no junk!" Jill retorted.

"We're not hatin. We just want you to slow down," said Mary.

"You know, Jill," Sandy jumped in, "Scripture says that even though Jesus was tempted—He didn't sin."

"Oh, so now I'm sinning?" laughed Jill. "You don't care; you just don't want to see a sista happy for a change."

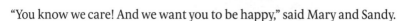

"You know we care! And we want you to be happy," said Mary and Sandy.

"But, we also care enough to tell you to slow down and be guided by the Holy Spirit and not your flesh!"

APPLICATION

Sometimes, temptation can be so strong we can't stand it! Think about one area in your life where you are tempted—whether the temptation is physical (like cigarettes, sex, or alcohol) or whether it's emotional (like gossiping or lying). Understand that Jesus sympathizes with our weakness in all areas. He understands because He was tempted with the same pressure we feel, yet He didn't sin. The secret to living a powerful life is to tap into God's power to overcome the temptation. Ask God to help you overcome temptation and provide a way of escape. Then trust, rely on, and believe that God rewards those who diligently seek Him.

DAY 5 / TASTE AND SEE THAT THE LORD IS GOOD!
MY BELLY IS FULL OF GOODNESS...

O taste and see that the Lord is good: blessed is the man
that trusteth in him.
Psalm 34:8

"Business is getting better and better every day," Stephanie bubbled over while talking with her business partner, Melody.

"Girl, you don't have to tell me that business is booming. We can't even keep up with the orders. I don't know what's happening, but I hope the trend continues. In fact, I wanted to talk with you about hiring some part-time help," Melody beamed.

"It's amazing," said Stephanie. "Ever since I decided that I was going to get serious about my prayer and study time in the Word, I've seen a change in my circumstances."

"Really? How?" asked Melody.

"Are you familiar with the Scripture, 'O taste and see that the Lord is good'"?

"Yes, Psalm 34:8," replied Melody.

"Well, I haven't had much goodness in my life, so I decided to 'taste' the goodness of the Lord through reading and mediating on His Word every day. And guess what? It works; my life has turned around!"

APPLICATION

The secret of seeing goodness in your life is to partake of God's goodness on a daily basis. Tasting the Word of God means to read Scripture with the intent of applying it to the current situations in your life.

Before you go to bed this evening, get a snack. As you're snacking, pull out your Bible and begin to read your favorite Scriptures. Snack and feast on the goodness of that Scripture and the goodness of your snack. Think about how good it will be when God answers your prayers.

PRAYER

Lord, I need to taste Your Word and experience Your goodness each day of my life. Teach me how to diligently pursue You in Your Word every day. Please have patience with me and have mercy on me. Show me Your kindness and Your goodness, Lord, every day of my life. In Jesus' name. Amen.

JANUARY

DAY 1 / CONFIDENCE IN SALVATION

DEATH IS ONLY THE BEGINNING!

"For God so loved the world, that he gave his only begotten Son, that whosoever believeth in him should not perish, but have everlasting life."
John 3:16

As far back as Deacon Smith could remember, there had never been a funeral that Mother Jackson had not attended. Not only did Mother Jackson faithfully attend funerals, but she seemed to enjoy them. While others would cry, Mother Jackson would sit quietly and rock side-to-side with a smile on her face.

One day, Deacon Smith asked her, "Mother Jackson, why do you seem to enjoy funerals so much?"

"A funeral is a happy occasion. Why shouldn't I enjoy them?" Mother Jackson answered.

"What do you mean happy occasion?" Deacon Smith asked confused.

"When a child of God dies, they are not lost. We know exactly where they are. They have gone home to glory to be with the Lord. While I'm sorry that their family members are sad, I know that as a child of God they are in a better place and one day the family will be reunited."

"You know, Deacon," said Mother Jackson with a wide smile on her face, "Everybody wanna go to heaven, but don't no one wanna die."

APPLICATION

As Christians, we must not live in fear of death. In John 14:2, Jesus told His disciples that He was going to prepare a place for them in heaven and He would return again to get them and take them there. And as children of the most high God, we too have a place waiting in heaven for us.

Today, help build someone's faith by telling them about Jesus and His promise of everlasting life.

PRAYER

Lord, thank You for Jesus and for the promise of everlasting life. Thank You for preparing a home for me in heaven. I will be confident in my salvation. I will not live in fear of death. I will live an abundant life while I am here on earth. Amen.

DAY 2 / CONFIDENCE IN PRAYER

I'VE GOT THE POWER!

*"And this is the confidence that we have in him, that, if we ask
any thing according to his will, he heareth us."*
1 John 5:14

" I swear God doesn't hear my prayers. I keep praying and asking God for solutions to our problems, but nothing is happening. Our finances are horrible, the kids are driving me crazy, and I still can't find a job. I don't think God is ever going to answer my prayers," Yvonne told her husband. "What am I doing wrong?"

Are you like Yvonne? Are you constantly praying and not getting any answers from God? If so, maybe your prayers go unanswered because you lack the confidence in God's ability to answer them. Too often, many Christians pray emotional, fear-based prayers that lack power. However, emotionalism doesn't get God's attention—only His Word does. God answers our prayers when we pray in accordance to His will and when we have the confidence (i.e., faith) to know that He will act.

APPLICATION

In order to effectively pray about your situation, it is critical for you to find out what God has said in the Bible about your situation. Today, begin to search the Bible for Scriptures that speak to an area in your life where you need help or desire change. Once you find those Scriptures, begin to meditate on them night and day. Place them in familiar places around your home and at your job, carry them around in your purse, and watch your prayers go from emotional and empty to positive and powerful.

PRAYER

Dear Lord, thank You for Your Word that teaches me Your will. I pray in the name of Jesus, according to Mark 11:24, that whatever I ask for in prayer according to Your will—will be granted. Amen.

DAY 3 / CONFIDENCE IN SELF
IT'S THE GOD IN ME!

"For the Lord shall be thy confidence, and shall keep thy foot from being taken."
Proverbs 3:26

❝It's the God in Me" is a song made popular by the gospel singing duo, Mary Mary. Conventional society will have us believe that self-confidence is how one succeeds in life. But that is not always the case. While many people attribute their success to their own efforts, sisters Tina and Erica Campbell (aka Mary Mary) remind us that the world is not our source. God is the source of our success.

God has provided for our needs through His blessings, of which there is a never-ending supply that exists for us, but we have to learn how to tap into them. Philippians 3:3 says that those who worship God in Spirit and have no confidence in the flesh are truly God's children.

APPLICATION

We all have the ability to succeed. The key is to stay connected to God. There are several ways to stay connected to God—from prayer, to reading and meditating on God's Word, to listening to Christian music. Today, purpose in your heart to stay connected to God by tapping into His never-ending supply of blessings for your life.

PRAYER

Lord, keep me humble and thankful in the knowledge that You are my source and I can do all things through Christ, who strengthens me. Amen.

DAY 4 / CONFIDENCE IN YOUR PURPOSE
AIN'T NO STOPPING ME NOW!

"Being confident of this very thing, that he which hath begun a good work in you will perform it until the day of Jesus Christ."
Philippians 1:6

One Sunday after morning worship, Sasha and her cousin Jackie went to breakfast. "Jackie, I don't think it's God's will for me to sing professionally. I've been trying for three years to land a paying job singing with no luck. Maybe I am only meant to sing with the praise and worship team at church," Sasha said with a sigh.

"Sasha, you are too talented to just give up. Just keep auditioning; God will open up the right door for you," Jackie encouraged.

"I don't know, Jackie. Maybe I should go to college to become a music teacher instead. At least that way I stand a chance to train a Broadway singer."

Before Jackie could respond, Sasha's cell phone rang. "Hello," she answered. Sasha remained silent. Jackie could not hear what the caller was saying. All of a sudden she saw tears streaming down her cousin's face.

"What's the matter, Sasha?" Jackie asked after Sasha had hung up.

"That was Pastor Todd. He said that a producer of a gospel play was at church this morning. The producer asked Pastor Todd to have me call because he thinks that I would be perfect for his upcoming production."

APPLICATION

Sometimes it can be difficult to wait on God to reveal His plan for our lives. Unfortunately, like Sasha, if we are not immediately successful in our endeavors, we think that our chosen path is not God's will for our life after all. We must have confidence that God created us for a purpose, and we cannot allow setbacks or temporary roadblocks to cause us to turn away from our destiny.

Today, determine to remain steadfast in the will of God for your life. Read and meditate on Psalm 32:8, which reads: "I will instruct you and teach you in the way you should go; I will guide you with My eye" (NKJV).

PRAYER

Lord, I pray that I will clearly hear the call You have on my life. Don't let me get sidetracked with things that are unessential to Your purpose. Lift my eyes above my circumstances so that I will not become discouraged by temporary inconveniences. Give me patience to wait for Your perfect timing. I am confident that You are the author and the finisher of my faith, and whatever You have placed in my heart will come to pass. Amen.

DAY 5 / CONFIDENCE THROUGH TRIALS
IT AIN'T OVER TILL I WIN!

"The Lord is my light and my salvation; whom shall I fear? The Lord is the strength of my life; of whom shall I be afraid? Though an host should encamp against me, my heart shall not fear: though war should rise against me, in this will I be confident."

Psalm 27:1, 3

For the past several weeks, Lauren's husband, Darnell has been working late. Even though Darnell says the reason for his lateness is because he's preparing contracts for a new account, Lauren suspects he's cheating on her with a new female executive that transferred in from another department. Rumor has it that she is notorious for flirting with her male counterparts. And, at six months pregnant, Lauren feels like she's losing her husband to an attractive, sexy woman. She feels unattractive and at a loss to compete with a high-powered female executive—she's lost all her confidence.

APPLICATION

Do you lack confidence? Do you see other women as beautiful while you think of yourself as merely alright looking? Do you feel less successful or intelligent, or doubt your ability to get things done? At some point, we all compare ourselves to others. In reality, it's pointless to compare yourself to others because doing so will always leave you feeling a sense of lack. Rather than comparing yourself to others, Paul says begin to measure yourself against God's standards (2 Corinthians 10:12). Don't look at the size or strength of your opponent. Instead, see yourself through God's eyes and focus on God's acceptance, security, and significance.

PRAYER

Lord, thank You for making me a partaker of Christ if I hold the beginning of my confidence steadfast to the end. Thank You for being my personal super hero, El Shaddai and for watching my back. Amen.

JANUARY

WEEK THREE: HEALTH AND HEALING

DAY 1 / NONE OF THESE DISEASES

NO, NOT ONE!

"And said, If thou wilt diligently hearken to the voice of the Lord thy God, and wilt do that which is right in his sight, and wilt give ear to his commandments, and keep all his statutes, I will put none of these diseases upon thee, which I have brought upon the Egyptians: for I am the Lord that healeth thee."

Exodus 15:26

Marilyn hung up the phone and sank into the chair in disbelief. "This cannot be happening," she said out loud. "Paula and I are the same age; we've been friends all of our lives. She is too young to have had a stroke. How could this have happened? What about her kids and her husband?"

In anguish, Marilyn cried out, "Dear God, why are your people suffering so much from conditions like strokes, diabetes, heart attacks, cancer? How could you let these things happen?"

APPLICATION

Sickness and disease don't just happen. In most cases, they are brought about as a result of people's disregard for eating right and maintaining a regular exercise routine. Upon closer look, it is more than likely that those individuals plagued by strokes, diabetes, and heart attacks ignore the warning sign that says, Get it together!

When God created Adam and Eve, He gave them the plan for healthy living (Genesis 1). He told them what to eat. He explained that the best exercise would be tending the garden in the fresh air and sunlight, and He sanctified the Sabbath and commanded them to rest (1:26—2:3). If they trusted His Word and yielded to Him—and stayed away from that tree—they would have health and happiness all their days. But Adam and Eve had another plan.

Is your lifestyle outside of God's plan for healthy living? If you or someone you know is suffering from a chronic illness, first follow the biblical recommendation in James 5:14-16 and offer up a prayer of faith to save the sick. Then get busy discovering what signs of poor health habits you may be ignoring and begin making a change today.

PRAYER

Creator of the universe, I am sorry for not honoring my body, Your temple, as I should. I humbly acknowledge my transgressions and ask that You create in me a clean heart (desire) and renew a right spirit within me. I ask that You heal me of all my diseases. Empower me by Your Holy Spirit to be obedient. Keep me alive and I will proclaim what You, O Lord, have done. Amen.

DAY 2 / TAKE TIME

I AIN'T GOT TIME, BABY...

"And every man that striveth for the mastery is temperate in all things."
1 Corinthians 9:25a

Lisa raced into the kitchen, grabbed her morning cup of coffee and car keys, and declared, "Okay, if I get out of here in two minutes, I'll make it to work on time."

As she rushed pass the babysitter, her six-year-old son Tre reached up and said, "Mommy, I want a hug."

"Tre," she answered, "I ain't got time, baby. If I stop now, I'll get stuck in traffic and be late for work!" And out the door she went.

The ride to work was a sobering one. What had she just done? How could she deny a warm and tender hug to the child that God had blessed her with? How had her life gotten to this point? How many other areas of her life were suffering because she was racing through life to get things done?

APPLICATION

The word temperate means avoiding that which is harmful and doing good things in moderation. It means knowing when to say "yes" and when to say "no." It means carefully looking at what God requires of us and at what the enemy dangles in front of us. It means discerning between a good idea and a God idea. It means sometimes being unpopular. It means choosing to set limits and stick to them. It means submitting to the Creator who really does know what is best for us and trusting Him to supply all of our needs according to His riches.

Take stock of the things that you are currently doing. List what you are currently focused on or responsible for—home, job, family, church, civic duties, and God. How much of what you are doing is really enhancing your life? Is there true balance in your life? Is there something (or things) that need changing? What will you do to make the changes?

PRAYER

Dear God, forgive me for being so caught up in "doing" that I am no longer "being." Please show me how to be temperate and bring balance to my life. Show me how to lay my yoke upon You because Your yoke is easy and Your burden is light. Thank You Jesus! Amen.

DAY 3 / EXERCISE YOUR OPTIONS
GET TO STEPPIN'...

"Jesus saith unto him, Rise, take up thy bed, and walk."
John 5:8

Red-eyed and weary, Pam stretched and looked at the clock—it was 3:00 am. "OMG! I need to take a sleeping pill and go to bed," she thought. "I need to look rested for my presentation in the morning."

Pam reached over and hit the snooze button—for the third time. "Ugh! Morning is here already; I just laid down at 3:00 a.m., and it's 7:00 a.m. already." Pam's days (and nights) were getting longer and longer; there were just not enough hours in a day. She had so much to do today. She had to prepare to give a presentation at work, pack her son Nicholas's lunch for school, make tonight's dinner, and to top it off she had to go with her mother to the eye doctor—all before she attended Nicholas's school program scheduled for tonight. "Guess I'll have a large double espresso this morning to get me started. And maybe tonight I'll take another sleeping pill to help me rest."

APPLICATION

Sound familiar? The hectic pace most women keep has gotten out of hand. Between the job, children, aging parents, and a husband, who has time to get proper rest? The sleeping pills we take to help us sleep and the caffeine-laden beverages we consume to wake us up do nothing more than lull us into thinking that we are feeling better than we actually feel and capable of doing it all. In reality, we are really tired; and when the drugs wear off, we are still sleep deprived and in dire need of rest.

How can we achieve that sweet, soul-refreshing rest—the kind that really prepares us for the day and the duties ahead? Jesus bids those who labor and are heavy laden to come to Him and He will give them rest (Matthew 11:28); so here's what you have to do:

Follow the Creator's example. _Plan time for rest._ On the seventh day, God rested from the work that He had done. _Plan time for exercise._ Get to steppin.... In the morning, arise, make up your bed, and take a walk outside! Start out doing what you can—just 10 to 20 minutes (even if it's indoors on a treadmill). You'll feel so much better. _Plan time to relax._ Tonight, turn off the cellphone. Put the kids in bed early, and put your spouse and friends on alert. Run a tub of water, light some candles, and soak in a nice hot bath. Or simply be still and meditate on God's Word, or read an inspirational book. Remember: "When thou liest down, thou shalt not be afraid: yea, thou shalt lie down and thy sleep shall be sweet" (Proverbs 3:24).

PRAYER

Lord, I want that sweet sleep. Help me today to make choices that will prepare my body for rest and rejuvenation. Teach me to relax and to rest in You. Amen.

COLLARD GREENS AND CORNBREAD...

"And God said, Behold, I have given you every herb bearing seed, which is upon the face of all the earth, and every tree, in the which is the fruit of a tree yielding seed; to you it shall be for meat."

Genesis 1:29

Beverly's class reunion was just two weeks away, and she really wanted to wear that red dress. Slowly, she took a deep breath and stepped into the dress. "This is ridiculous," she thought. "I won't be able to enjoy myself squeezed up like this. Those pills I was taking didn't burn anything but a hole in my wallet! And those diets don't work either. What am I gonna do?"

APPLICATION

Fruits, nuts, and grains comprised the first diet given to us by God. Scientists today are discovering that God's original diet for man really is best. Surprisingly, some of the best foods to eat are black-eyed peas, brown rice, collard greens (cooked without the fat-back, of course), sweet potatoes, and cornbread. Jeremiah 46:11 says, "In vain shalt thou use many medicines, for thou shalt not be cured." Taking diet pills and going on crash diets is only a temporary fix to help you fit into that special occasion dress. But in the long run, the short cut is really damaging to your health.

Choose today to adopt a diet that promotes health and protects against disease, and start meditating on Scriptures like: "Whether therefore ye eat, or drink...do all to the glory of God" (1 Corinthians 10:31). Eat three good meals a day (making the third one very light). Eliminate snacks, and drink plenty of water. Keep that special outfit out where you can see it. You'll be wearing it again soon!

PRAYER

Dear God, I don't want quick fixes for my health. I want long-term solutions. Help me take control of my appetite. Take control of my hunger, and help me to align my diet with foods designed for me and my family's health and well being. In Jesus' name. Amen.

DAY 5 / MOSTLY WATER
NEVER THIRST AGAIN...

"And let him that is athirst come. And whosoever will, let him drink take the water of life freely."
Revelation 22:17b

"Hey babe," Karen called to her husband, Charles. "I'm so thirsty. Can you please pour me something to drink?" A few seconds later, Charles handed Karen a glass of ice cold lemonade. As she gulped down the last drop, Karen realized that this was her fourth beverage today, and the weird thing was nothing she drank really quenched her thirst.

Since our bodies are about three-fourths water, it is vitally important to keep giving ourselves a fresh supply. Water carries chemicals throughout the body, aids in the digestion of food, purifies the blood, invigorates body organs, regulates body temperatures, increases blood circulation, and increases red and white blood cell count. No other liquid provides nourishment for the body like water does—not soda, coffee, Kool-Aid, lemonade, punch, or milk. Yet, we constantly drink beverages filled with sugar and caffeine and wonder why our thirst is never quenched.

Maybe we are like the woman at the well—standing in front of the answer to our problem and not recognizing it. Jesus told the woman that if she knew who He was, she would have asked water of Him and He would have given her living water.

APPLICATION

Get a 16-ounce bottle, fill it with water three times a day, and drink it in between meals throughout the day. Don't wait until you're thirsty. By the time you feel thirsty, you're already dehydrated. As you drink the water, remember that drinking freely from Jesus' well that never runs dry is guaranteed to quench your thirst.

PRAYER

Lord, I'm tired of drinking and not quenching my thirst. Today, I will choose to drink more water, physically and spiritually. I also choose to dip my spiritual cup deep into the well of Your Word so that my soul will be satisfied and I will never thirst again. Amen.

JANUARY

WEEK FOUR: SELF ESTEEM

DAY 1 / NO ACCIDENTS

WHO AM I?

"So God created man in his own image."
Genesis 1:27a

Shelly stood looking at her swollen face in the mirror wondering, "Who Am I? How did I get here? Am I special to anybody?" Somehow Shelly had gotten herself involved in a relationship with an abusive man. At first, everything was good. He took her out to nice places. He bought her flowers. He treated her with kindness and care. She thought he was the "one." But suddenly the verbal abuse started, which quickly turned into physical abuse. Shelly was at a loss to figure out how things could have deteriorated so quickly. "Who am I?" she thought. "Who is this person staring back at me in the mirror?" she questioned as the tears streamed down her face.

It's not uncommon for women who are in abusive or demeaning relationships, or who have simply made bad relationship decisions to feel depressed, inadequate, unattractive, unloved, unwanted, and of no value. Out of shame, they might even go so far as to distance themselves from others. Adam and Eve did the same thing. After they ate the apple, sin, guilt, and fear caused them to feel unpresentable and unworthy to be in the presence of the One who loved them.

Everyone yearns for a sense of belonging, a sense of worth. We want to feel good about ourselves and to know that others feel the same about us. We want to know that we matter, that our living is worthwhile and has direction. Knowing that there is an awesome God who created you in His image stimulates a proud feeling. So, the next time you stand looking in the mirror asking yourself, "Who am I?" you can joyously respond by saying, "I am the creation of a perfectly awesome God who made me in His image for a purpose. Indeed, I do matter; and I am worthwhile."

APPLICATION

In order to have positive self-esteem, you must understand who you are. Take a moment to meditate on the image of an awesome God making and shaping you to be just exactly as you are. Write down five characteristics, features, or emotions that God made unique to you. Then take time to thank God for making you who you are.

PRAYER

Father, You made me in Your image, perfectly and wondrously. Help me to know that deep down in my spirit and soul. I also know that You created me for a purpose. I ask that You reveal my purpose to me. Lord, help me to understand who I am. In Jesus' name. Amen.

DAY 2 / YOURSELF

WHO DO I THINK THAT I AM?

"I will praise thee; for I am fearfully and wonderfully made: marvellous are thy works; and that my soul knoweth right well."

Psalm 139:14

Dark chocolate, honey-colored, or eggnog-shaded complexion. Hips full as water balloons or flat as a tire. Twig legs or tree trunks. Sassy mouth or quiet as a church mouse. God beautifully created all of us in His image using different sizes, shapes, and complexions.

We may have been created in God's image, but that's not always how we see ourselves. What do you see when you look into the mirror: a raving beauty or a wretched, miserable being? The fact is that beauty is not just about how you look on the outside; it's about being beautiful on the inside.

Do you feel good about yourself? Is there guilt, shame, condemnation, or fear clouding your self-image? At some point, every woman has asked themselves these types of questions. We ask them because we want to understand our purpose in life, our place, and our worth. Thankfully, God's love is boundless. That means we don't ever have to hide or feel ashamed about who we are or how we look. We are a beautiful image of the creation that God lovingly created.

APPLICATION

In order to have a positive self-image, you must feel good about yourself. You have to love yourself. For today, add to the list of unique characteristics from yesterday. Write down five more characteristics that you would like to acquire and another five for areas you'd like to change. Put the list in a place where you can see it each day for the rest of the week. Meditate on the list throughout the week.

PRAYER

Father, I ask You to help me see the great gifts, talents, beauty, and character that I possess—not for the sake of pride, but for Your glory. Forgive me for my sins; and remove any depression, guilt, shame, condemnation, or inadequacy from me because I know that it doesn't come from You. Help me to love myself as You love me. In Jesus' name. Amen.

WHO DO OTHERS THINK THAT I AM?

"And he said, Who told thee that thou wast naked?"
Genesis 3:11a

Shanice was excited to be going to her 20-year high school reunion. She had purchased a really nice outfit for the "meet and greet" reception and took extra time to get her hair just right. As she took one last check in the mirror, she thought everything was perfect. She left the house feeling good, looking good, and even smelling good.

When she arrived at the reunion, the first person she encountered was her old rival, Denise. As Denise approached her, she gave her a snarling look and rolled her eyes and said, "Hey girl, long time no see. That's an interesting outfit you're wearing—not a nice outfit, but an 'interesting' one—and you look different with short hair."

"What does 'different' mean?" Shanice thought. All of a sudden, she went from feeling great about herself to doubting her hair and outfit choices.

Others don't always see you the way you see yourself. There are times when the input, comments, and suggestions from others are true, needful, and intended to encourage and uplift you. But there are also times when the intent is to hurt or demean you because, often, hurting people hurt others. You must be able to discern the difference. A good rule of thumb is that God aims to strengthen you and build you up, not tear you down.

If another's comments are not offered in love or the intent is to tear you down, don't take their comments to heart.

Adam and Eve were hiding in shame when they told God that they were naked. God asked them, "Who told you that you were naked?" (Genesis 3:11, NIV). He wanted to know how they could have been deceived into believing that they were unworthy of His presence and love because of how they looked.

APPLICATION

People will always judge and have opinions, but you must be able to take the comments of others and compare them to who God says you are: a creation made in His image. Pull out your list. Write down five characteristics you think others see in you that you agree with, and then compare that list with who God says you are. God's list will win out every time!

PRAYER

Father, I know that You are God and that no mean word or action against me is stronger than Your love for me. I ask that You don't let the arrows and snares of others penetrate the positive words that You've spoken about me. I pray that You teach me how to forgive those who are spiteful and mean to me and want to hurt or belittle me. In Jesus' name. Amen.

WHO DOES GOD SAY THAT I AM?

*"Since thou wast precious in my sight, thou hast been honourable,
and I have loved thee."*

Isaiah 43:4a

How would you feel if you had a father who was well-known, powerful, and highly regarded around the world? What if he also had a staff too large to number that was available at his beck and call? What if he could fix every problem and provide every single thing that you will ever need, and he loved you with an everlasting love? Wouldn't it make you feel good to have such a father? Well, you do—in your heavenly Father; and He sees you as His treasured possession—a precious, fine jewel.

God says that we belong to Him. Sometimes we get caught up in financial struggles, physical battles, marital troubles, professional woes, family crises, and on and on. In the midst of those situations, we forget whose we are. We are God's adopted children, a peculiar people who have the same rights and privileges as His only Son, Jesus. When we don't know whose we are, we can easily settle for so much less than what God wants for us. The good news is that God doesn't beat you over the head with your shortcomings. He doesn't judge you or see you the way others do. He sees you as His precious creation and loves you enough to have sacrificed His beloved Son so that you might have life more abundantly. Now that's not a bad family to be in.

APPLICATION

You are precious to God. Pull out the list you've been working on this week, and write down five reasons why God is special to you.

PRAYER

Father God, I now know that You love me and that You are willing to move heaven and hell on my behalf. I know that You love me so much that You sacrificed Your Son so that I might be free. Help me feel the confidence and certainty of knowing that I am Your child and You love me unconditionally. Amen.

DAY 5 / KEEP GOD'S PERSPECTIVE

I AM!

"Before I formed thee in the belly I knew thee; and before thou camest forth out of the womb I sanctified thee, and I ordained thee a prophet unto the nations."

Jeremiah 1:5

You are exactly who God created you to be. You are uniquely made with just the right complexion, body shape, height, hair texture, emotions, and desires. You were no accident or mistake. God had a plan and purpose for you even before you were born. How awesome it is to know that your heavenly Father wants you. You are the apple of your Father's eye.

Your heavenly Father loves you so much. You are a treasured possession that He handles with great care. He wipes your shortcomings, sin, and guilt sparkling clean with the blood of redemption and restoration through the power of repentance. Never view yourself through the judgmental eyes of others; rather, see yourself through the proud fatherly eyes of God as the wonderful, beautiful image that He created. Walk in the confidence that you are the apple in the almighty King's eye. You are because He is.

APPLICATION

As joint-heirs with the Son of God, Christ Jesus, you are entitled to the best. Take the list you've created this week and create a series of "I AM" statements to remind you of how valuable, special, and beautiful you are to the Lord. Boldly confess the "I AM" statements every day to remind yourself that you are His chosen, predestined, and treasured possession.

PRAYER

Father, thank You for Your love. From this day forward, I will not let myself or others make me feel less than the royal princess that I am. I will no longer let the words or actions of others or even my own thoughts rob me of the joy and favor that You have poured into my life. From this day forward, I will seek to fulfill the purpose that You've established for my life—that You might be glorified. Thank You for creating me just as I am—the apple of Your eye. In Jesus' name. Amen.

JANUARY

WEEK FIVE: SUCCESS

DAY 1 / SUCCESS IN CHRIST

THERE IS PLENTY TO GO AROUND!

"This book of the law shall not depart out of thy mouth; but thou shalt meditate therein day and night, that thou mayest observe to do according to all that is written therein: for then thou shalt make thy way prosperous, and then thou shalt have good success."

Joshua 1:8

Kelly was on the fast track at work. Three promotions in two years had her perfectly positioned to become partner with the consulting firm where she worked. Kelly's business world was based on survival of the fittest, and she honestly believed that the Lord wanted her to be successful at her career.

One Sunday at church Kelly's pastor preached about discovering one's divine purpose in life. Kelly figured she knew hers, but she decided to pray with the congregation anyway. She asked God how she should be using her life to serve Him.

When Kelly walked away from her career a year later to become a missionary at a small religious school in Haiti, she knew she had done the right thing. When asked by her family and friends if she regretted giving up her career, she quickly replied, "I didn't give up my career; I just traded up for a new one!"

APPLICATION

Oftentimes, what seems like a detour in life serves as God's way of setting us up for another type of success. Success isn't calculated by how much money you earn or how many things you acquire. Success comes in following the lead of God and allowing the Holy Spirit to order your steps.

Mother Teresa is quoted as saying, "Wherever God has put you that is your vocation. It is not what we do, but how much love we put into what we do." Reflect on your life today and ask yourself, "What is God's purpose for my life?" If you know the answer, then share your experiences with others who are still seeking their purpose. If you don't know the answer to the question, then make it a priority today to pray that it will be revealed to you.

PRAYER

Lord, I want to live for You. I want my life to be a reflection of Your will for me. Help me to know the purpose for my life. Give me the courage to embrace Your answer, and take away any fear or doubt that would keep me from successfully living for You. In Jesus' name. Amen.

DAY 2 / PERSONAL SUCCESS
I THINK I CAN, I THINK I CAN!

"Wherefore seeing we also are compassed about with so great a cloud of witnesses, let us lay aside every weight, and the sin which doth so easily beset us, and let us run with patience the race that is set before us, Looking unto Jesus the author and finisher of our faith; who for the joy that was set before him endured the cross, despising the shame, and is set down at the right hand of the throne of God."

Hebrews 12:1-2

Doreen and Wesley were the most prepared first-time parents imaginable. They had read every book, gone to every website, and had even taken an online course on childbirth and parenting; but when the time came to give birth, the pain Doreen felt was enough to send her through the roof. She kept thinking, "What is up with this? Women give birth every day! Isn't this supposed to be a natural thing? Why does it hurt so badly?" By the third hour of labor, Doreen was sleep deprived and ready for a caesarian section. Doreen cried and prayed, "Lord, I am doing my best, and I can't take this pain anymore. I want to have a caesarian. Please give me the strength to hold on."

Shortly after her prayer, Wesley entered the birthing room and began encouraging her. He told her she had the strength of Jesus in her and that she could do all things through Him. He reminded Doreen that her grandmother had birthed seven children and her mother three. He reinforced the importance of what Doreen was doing, which gave her the strength to hold on. By morning, Doreen and Wesley were parents to little Daja, a 7 pound, 8 ounce baby girl.

APPLICATION

Doreen was given a new outlook on having the spiritual strength to press on. Today's Scripture in Hebrews 12 explains that heaven is watching us in our trials and that even when obstacles get in the way we are encouraged to patiently continue the race using Jesus' endurance on the Cross as our example.

Can you do all things through Christ? Yes, you can! The next time you meet an insurmountable challenge, before you say, "I can't do it," take a deep breath and ask Christ for the strength to try. Once you're in the midst of trying, pray and ask God for the strength to finish. You will be surprised at how much you can accomplish once you confess your God-given strength.

PRAYER

Heavenly Father, thank You for reminding me that You always know what's best for me. Help me to stay energized for the task at hand and to reach my goals. Remind me daily that my personal success can only be measured by You. In your eyes, I am always a winner. Amen.

DAY 3 / A SUCCESSFUL FAMILY
FAMILY FIRST AND FOREMOST...

*"That they may teach the young women to be sober,
to love their husbands, to love their children, To be discreet,
chaste, keepers at home, good, obedient to their own husbands,
that the word of God be not blasphemed."*
Titus 2:4-5

Gordon and Tamika rent a small office where they run a business. Within the space they created a playroom for their son Gabriel. One of the reasons they decided to start a business was because they wanted to have to home school their children. Oftentime clients, upon hearing a child in the background, would open up quickly and begin to tell them about their own children. Never once did anyone make a negative comment about the baby crying, laughing, or cooing in the workplace. In fact, people usually delight in the fact that they have the opportunity to keep their child with them as they operate their business.

Friends ask them if it's difficult to raise an infant and run a business at the same time. Their answer is, "Yes, but it is more rewarding than we could have ever expected!" Tamika delights in the knowledge that both her spouse and her child are getting the attention and love they need; and in return, she is pleasing God by honoring His command.

APPLICATION

Today's Scripture is a blueprint for how godly women should strive to achieve a Christ-centered family life. If you are married with young children or expecting a new arrival, if possible, consider staying home with your children during their early years or at least for the first year of life. One of your greatest duties is raising your children. At first it may seem impossible to survive on one income, but remain prayerful and devise a financial plan in advance .Unfortunately, single parents may not have the luxury of staying home to raise a child, but you too should look closely at your life and make sure your commitments to work, school, church, or other activities are not overshadowing your commitment to your children.

PRAYER

Father God, I will always make family my priority. I know that You have called me to be a godly woman, and I will do everything possible to let my light shine through my family. Give me the wisdom to make the right decisions concerning my family. Amen.

DAY 4 / SUCCESS IN LIFE

YOU GOTTA HAVE FAITH!

"For we walk by faith, not by sight."
2 Corinthians 5:7

"I'll believe it when I see it" or "seeing is believing" are familiar expressions to us all. However, it is faith that allows us to see the unseen. Today's Scripture, while simple, is one of the boldest in the Bible. It is a life-changing statement that, if put into action, can have overwhelming results.

Have you ever played the trust game at a retreat or at camp? Here's how it works. You turn your back toward your partner, close your eyes, and trust that when you fall backward he or she will catch you. It takes a lot of faith to believe that this person will have the physical strength to catch you and not allow you to land on the floor, but that's exactly what God is asking of you. If you could play the trust game with a person, just think how great your relationship with God could be when you close your eyes, let go, fully trust Him, and allow yourself to fall back into His arms?

APPLICATION

Do you trust God to take care of every area in your life? In the Greek, the word walk in today's Scripture means to live. In other words, Paul is making a bold statement that all believers (like the Corinthians) should be living by faith and not simply by what they

221

see. Reflect on a time when you had to trust and believe God until a bad situation got better. What did you learn about yourself during that time? What did you learn about God? What situation are you currently "seeing" in your life that may be causing you to doubt God's plan or purpose for your life? What steps can you take to start believing in those things you can't see?

PRAYER

Lord, be patient with me as I work to increase my faith. I realize that in a world filled with anxiety, conflict, problems, and fear, faith is essential for my survival. I will be faithful today to myself, faithful to my obligations and commitments, and faithful to You. Amen.

DAY 5 / ALL AROUND SUCCESS
BALANCING IT ALL

"Thou wilt keep him in perfect peace, whose mind is stayed on thee: because he trusteth in thee."

Isaiah 26:3

Roxanne used to be the queen of making "to-do" lists. Her daily list was color-coded, time-stamped, and meticulously detailed down to the smallest activity of her day. Even though every self-help book on success swears by them, Roxanne finally stopped keeping an official "to-do" list. It had become too stressful and depressing to see how many things were left undone at the end of a day. The day she stopped beating herself up for not making it to the end of her "to-do" list and started trusting God with her day was the day she felt free from self-criticism and unnecessary obligations. Every now and then when she feels extremely overwhelmed, she is tempted to get on her computer and begin a list; but she quickly dismisses the thought and returns to trusting God to help her meet any crises and challenges as they arise.

APPLICATION

There is no "to-do" list concerning the peace of God. The key to achieving perfect peace is simply to keep our minds settled on God. If we trust Jesus and keep our mind focused on Him, God promises that we can achieve perfect peace. Different people do this in different ways. Some people pray. Some people journal their thoughts. Others read the Bible. One way that works for me is meditation. Meditation allows you to operate in a realm of peace and tranquility to meet the challenges of your day head on. Seek out Scripture on which you can meditate, put on some tranquil music, and find a quiet spot in your home—whatever it takes to help you to clear your mind and focus on God's Word. Start with 5 or 10 minutes a day and build toward a goal of 20 or 30 minutes every morning. You will be surprised how the simple act of being still each morning will set you up for a peaceful day.

PRAYER

Lord, give me a clear and uncluttered mind so that I can be at perfect peace today and every day, even in the midst of a storm. Help me to slow down so that I can hear the answers to my prayers and receive Your blessings. In Jesus' name. Amen.

WEEK 1: DATING

DAY 1 / KEYS TO SUCCESSFUL DATING

GO OUT WITH GOD...

*"The simple believeth every word: but the prudent man
looketh well to his going."*
Proverbs 14:15

Chante was over 30 and all of her friends were married, engaged, or involved in serious relationships, she felt as if she was being left behind. So, when she met Tremaine she allowed herself to get romantically involved with him before really getting to know him. When Tremaine's bad habits and unpleasant tendencies revealed themselves she ignored them. For example, Chante believed in saving for the future; Tremaine didn't, he believed in living for the moment. Chante was a people person, she was active in several ministries at church and she belonged to several social clubs. Tremaine, on the other hand, rarely attended church, never wanted to socialize and he seemed uncomfortable around people he didn't know very well. Still Chante continued to date him hoping that one day he would change. Despite their vast differences eventually the courtship led to a walk down the aisle. Within the first year their marriage was in shambles and divorce was imminent.

APPLICATION

Communication is a very important part of dating. Divorce rates in the U.S. have been rising rapidly. A few of the reasons for the increase can be attributed to incompatibility between couples, infidelity, and financial pressures, most of which can be attributed to lack of communication.

If you find that you and your significant other are seeking different things or are on different paths, do not ignore the signs thinking things will improve. Prior to considering marriage it's best to seek pre-marital counseling, preferably Christian pre-marital counseling. Don't expect your date to change his way of thinking just because you want him to. Pray and invite God into your relationship and seek His wisdom in your quest to find the perfect mate for you.

PRAYER

Heavenly Father, give me the strength to see myself the way that you do and the wisdom to recognize the mate that you have for me. If this man is not the one for me, please give me the courage to end the relationship and wait on the mate you have for me. Amen.

DAY 2 / IS THE LOVE THAT YOU FEEL REAL?

HOW DO YOU KNOW?

"How fair is thy love, my sister, my spouse! How much better is thy love than wine! And the smell of thine ointments than all spices!"
Song of Solomon 4:10

How do you know if you're in love? First of all, love isn't selfish. Second, if you care just as much for the other person's happiness as you do for your own, you consistently show a willingness to make sacrifices for another and you actively work toward settling differences out of the deep respect you have for one another, then chances are you're probably in love.

The love promoted in books, on television, and at the movies tends to be distorted. If you are experiencing feelings of uncontrollable desire, selfishness, or lack confidence and trust in your mate, chances are you're not in love and may just be infatuated.

The Bible speaks extensively about the power of love. The story of Jacob and Rachel vividly illustrates genuine love in the Bible. The Song of Solomon is a celebration of romantic love and reminds us of love as God intended. First Corinthians 13 describes unfailing love, and Ephesians 5:25-33 discusses the love that men ought to show toward their wives.

APPLICATION

Before you decide whether what you're feeling is love, consider these points:

* Are you always thinking; "What's in this relationship for me?"

* Are you overly interested in the other person's physical appearance?

* Are you ignoring negative signs about the other person's personality traits?

* Are arguments frequent and nothing really gets settled?

If you answered yes to any of these questions it's possible that what you're feeling is not be true love. Love is intimate, unselfish, committed, and faithful. Love is when you recognize his faults, yet you love him anyway. If you are attracted to his entire personality (both his physical and his spiritual qualities), and during times of disagreements are you able to talk them out and settle them peaceably —then you are well on your way to a loving, caring relationship.

PRAYER

Heavenly Father, please grant me the wisdom to recognize the differences between real love and infatuation. Help me to remember that genuine love grows stronger with time and provides for a perfect union with the right man. Amen.

DAY 3 / SEX AND THE SINGLE WOMAN

KEEP COOL!

"I say therefore to the unmarried and widows, It is good for them if they abide even as I. But if they cannot contain, let them marry: for it is better to marry than to burn."

1 Corinthians 7: 8-9

Denise and Gerald had been dating for the past 6 months and enjoyed each other's company. However, for the past few weeks, Gerald had been pressuring her to take their relationship to the "next level" by engaging in sex. When Denise insisted that she wanted to wait for the man who would be her husband, Gerald countered by saying he planned to marry her in the future if things worked out between them.

Denise couldn't deny that she really liked this man and was curious about what an intimate sexual relationship with Gerald would be like. Still, she desired to honor God by remaining faithful and abstaining from sex until marriage. For the next month or so Gerald continued to pressure her for sex, but when she would bring up the subject of marriage, he argued that he could never marry a woman without knowing whether or not they would be compatible sexually. Despite his threats to end the relationship, Denise held her ground. A few days later, Gerald ended the relationship. The breakup was painful for Denise, but she found peace because she realized two things: 1) her virginity like, like a diamond, is valuable and rare, and 2) If Gerald was willing to break up with her because she desired to follow God's will, he was NOT the man for her.

APPLICATION

As Christians, the temptation toward sexual sin is greatest when we are involved in a committed relationship. It's only natural to want to feel loved and physical intimacy is an expression of that love. Unfortunately, most couples make the mistake of engaging in physical intimacy too soon and justify the behavior by telling themselves, "If we love each other, it's all right." However, the reality is, sex alone cannot forge a lasting relationship between couples. Often when that happens, meaningful conversation ceases and potential relationship problems get glossed over temporarily hidden by physical arousal only to resurface later in the relationship.

Remaining chaste before marriage is not an easy thing to accomplish; but for those who choose to wait they experience the peace of knowing that they are pleasing God. From the beginning of the courtship, let your date know what your attitude is regarding sex. Set limits on expressions of affection without sending out mixed signals. Avoid tempting situations and know your own limitations.

PRAYER

Heavenly Father, please give me wisdom to know my own limitations when it comes to dating. I ask for the strength to say no and mean it. Give me power beyond what is normal to remain chaste. I know that I can do it with your help and blessing. Amen.

DAY 4 / THE DARK SIDE OF DATING
SEXUAL ASSAULT...

"Fear thou not; for I am with thee: be not dismayed; for I am thy God: I will strengthen thee; yea, I will help thee; yea, I will uphold thee with the right hand of my righteousness."

Isaiah 41: 10

Rebecca and Pierce had been dating for almost a year and had become engaged. This night was no different from any other night, or so Rebecca thought. When Pierce announced he'd left his wallet home and had to stop off at his apartment, she didn't think anything of it. When they arrived, Pierce insisted that Rebecca accompany him, saying that he feared for her safety alone in the car.

Rebecca entered the apartment and Pierce called for her to join him in his bedroom. She did so without reserve. It wasn't until he pushed her down on the bed that she started to worry. When he hit her, Rebecca began to fear for her life. He raped her before taking her home. She called off the wedding and pressed charges, despite feeling that no one would believe that the nice young man she'd intended to marry could do something like this.

She went on with her life, but she struggled with her relationship with God. How could he have let this happen? Wasn't he supposed to take care of her?

When grief from a traumatic event overshadows you, you may start to question the very presence of God in your life. Blinded by your losses, you neither feel nor see the favor of God. You trusted God to take care of you; yet he allowed you to become victim of this terrible evil. Trusting him is just not that simple anymore. Your relationship with God has changed.

Nothing can alter what happened—you can only change how you deal with what has occurred. There are only two choices: You can go through your crisis with God, or you can go through it without him. Many victims abandon prayer following an assault, but only through prayer can you start to sense the healing presence of God throughout your recovery.

APPLICATION

We are supposed to forgive the people who hurt us. Forgiving does not mean that we forget. Neither does it mean that we excuse what happened. We have to hold rapists accountable and take them to court. But when we truly have forgiven the person who has hurt us, we no longer harbor malice in our hearts. It is only through forgiveness that we will find peace.

PRAYER

Heavenly Father, please replace my discouragement with hope and help me to release my anger in ways that do not create more damage. Furthermore, please replace my disappointment in you with a desire to communicate with you. Although I am the one who must choose to forgive, I know that forgiveness is only accomplished through you and your Word. Amen.

DAY 5 / MENDING A BROKEN HEART

CHANGE, NOT REJECTION...

"A time to get, and a time to lose; a time to keep,
and a time to cast away."

Ecclesiastes 3: 6

When Greg asked Karla to marry him, it was a dream come true for her. They had been dating for three years, and she was more than ready for marriage. Greg had been married before but this would be her first. Months passed and the closer it came to their wedding day, the stranger Greg acted. He and Karla argued frequently—especially when she tried to discuss wedding plans. Every time Karla would begin to have doubts, she would glance down at the ring on her finger. Greg proposed—therefore, he wanted to get married, she reasoned.

Two weeks before the wedding, after invitations had gone out, Greg came to see her. He announced that he wanted to call off the wedding. Although Karla had suspected as much for weeks, nothing prepared her for the heartache that followed. Greg wanted to end the relationship. He cared for her but didn't love her the way a husband should love a wife. Waves of humiliation swept through her as she considered what would have to be done. On its heels, anger rolled in. It was weeks before Karla was able to function without shedding a tear, but she was determined to move on with her life. However, Greg's rejection had soured her view of future relationships.

Along with dating comes the very strong possibility of rejection. There are no guarantees that love will grow. When a relationship dies, usually an explosion of tears or anger follows. Even when a breakup is handled with the utmost tact and kindness, you are still bound to experience feelings of rejection, hurt and outrage. Your self-esteem may even be under attack.

You have a right to let the other person know how you feel but emotional ranting and raving accomplishes little. There is also no need for you to humiliate yourself by begging and pleading for the affections of a person who obviously has few feelings for you. If you find that someone is using you, then it's better to end the relationship. It may still be painful, though.

There will be times when you may be plagued with memories or tormented by loneliness. It's okay to have a good cry. It also helps to spend time with friends and family or to stay busy. In between relationships, use this time to work on certain aspects of your personality. Your idea of a mate may be clearer after having loved and lost. Deciding what went wrong in previous relationships will serve as a guide when you start dating again.

APPLICATION

Look in the mirror and tell yourself that the fact that you were not desirable in one person's eyes does not mean that you will not be desirable in the eyes of someone else. It is better to wait for the right man—the one sent by God.

PRAYER

Heavenly Father, help me to keep my mind on you during this time of heartache. I know that you have someone better in mind for me and I thank you in advance. Give me strength during this difficult time. Amen.

FEBRUARY
WEEK TWO: LOVE

DAY 1 / LOVE OF GOD
MY CREATOR, MY SAVIOR, MY LORD...

"In the beginning God created the heaven and the earth."
Genesis 1:1

How many times have we given our love to people who did not want it, to people who did not appreciate it, and to people who just abused it because they could? Consider a loving God, our heavenly Father, who has promised to always love us, never to leave us, and never to forsake us. He loves us so much that He sent his only Son to walk among us so that He could know our pain and our suffering, and so that He could identify with our sinful nature. He took our sin to the Cross, separating Himself from his Father at that point, so that we might live. This is the epitome of love; while we were yet sinners, Christ died for us. That's GOOD NEWS!

APPLICATION

Women of color begin each day thanking God for your salvation and tell Him how much you love Him. Tell him how good and how great He is. Praise Him for being the Rose of Sharon, the Bright and Morning Star, the Prince of Peace—He is altogether lovely. When you learn to esteem God on a daily basis, God is rewarder of those who diligently seek Him.

PRAYER

This is the day that the Lord has made; I will rejoice and be glad in it. I will bless the Lord at all times. His praise shall continually be in my mouth. Father, in the name of Jesus, I adore you and I love you. It is in the wonderful name of Jesus I pray, Amen.

DAY 2 / LOVE OF SELF

IF I CAN'T LOVE ME, THEN WHO CAN I LOVE?

"I will praise thee; for I am fearfully and wonderfully made."
Psalm 139:14

As children in Sunday School, many of us learned the familiar song, "Yes, Jesus Loves Me." When we sang it we believed it. Then, as time moved on and life's disappointments came along and we stopped believing what we first learned about God's love for us. Sometimes it's hard to imagine that God loves us so much, but He does. At some point, we've all fallen victim to the world's definition of love. Pop culture would have us believe that in order to be loved we should wear our hair a certain way, dress a certain way, maintain a certain weight or a certain image. The devil is a lie! The fact is, throughout scripture, God demonstrates his unwavering love and admiration for us— despite of us. God made each one of us special and unique in our own way.

God created us the way we are for a reason. We should never feel pressure to conform to what others say or think about us because God didn't make us like other people. From Rahab (Joshua 2—6), to the woman who committed adultery (John 8:1-12), to Mary, the mother of Jesus, nothing can separate us from the love of God (Rom. 8:38). These women were not perfect, they were flawed. They had experienced some of life's most difficult situations; yet they were fearfully and wonderfully made and God loved them (and used them mightly) just the way they were!

APPLICATION

Ladies, learn to love you again! Never try and live your life based on how other people think you should look or on what other people think you should do. Today, begin to search the Word of God and find every Scripture that talks about how much God loves you and about how precious you are in His eyes. Read them over and over until they take root in your mind and your heart. Make it personal and then share what God says about you with another sister. When you build others up, God will build you up.

PRAYER

Father God, thank You for fearfully and wonderfully creating me. Thank You that for loving me just the way I am. Free from the spirit of low self-esteem, the spirit of defeat, the spirit of confusion, the spirit of poverty, and every other spirit that is not of You. Thank you for reminding me that "Yes, Jesus loves me! In Jesus' Name, Amen.

DAY 3 / LOVE OF MATE

A GOOD THING!

"Create in me a clean heart, O God; and renew a right spirit within me."

Psalm 51:10

As Christian women, in particular, we've all had fantasies about what life would be like when the Lord sent the husband we prayed for—that is until we got married. It's a fact, getting married is easy, but marriage is hard. Are you finding that there is a bit of a frog in your Prince Charming? Are you having difficulty being the "good thing" the bible talks about in Proverbs 18:22? Well, I'm certain you are not alone!

Learning to love our mates in the good times and in the bad times is difficult. Our minds have to be changed so that our hearts can be changed. If you have forgiven him, please show your love. How many times and how often is he going to have to pay for the same mistake? Relationships that accept God's grace and forgiveness persevere through life's difficulties. As you remain committed to the promise that you made to your mate and in the sight of God, God will be faithful. What God has joined together, let no man or woman put asunder. Love, my sisters, is an action word, and love, my sisters, never fails.

APPLICATION

Women of color, love your mates for the men of God that they are at this time in their lives. Support their efforts and their ideas. Trust me, it's easier to regroup after a good plan has gone bad, than it is to mend a broken spirit because you didn't believe in him. Tell your husband that he is the only man on this planet that you could have married.

Dear Heavenly Father, Thank you for my good husband. I am most blessed, Lord. I pray for those who are seeking a good mate, that they will be guided by Your Holy Spirit and find just the right person with whom they will share their lives. Lord, I also pray for those who are already married and ask that you strengthen the good marriages and heal those marriages that have suffered wounds and hurts. May each mate seek more of Your love and be willing to lay down their lives for each other. Let us all be filled with more of Your love daily. May love pour from me today no matter what I face. I ask this in the name of the Lord, Jesus Christ. Amen.

PRAYER

Father God, in the name of Jesus, forgive us for not always showing love to our mates, for being manipulative in our giving, and for keeping an account of everything that we think is wrong. Oh God, I thank you for reminding me that love keeps no records of wrongs. Lord, I purpose on this day to be a better wife than I was yesterday. Thank you, Lord, for my husband. In Jesus' Name, Amen.

CLOSE ENCOUNTERS OF THE FAMILY KIND...

"For ye have not received the spirit of bondage again to fear; but ye have received the spirit of adoption, whereby we cry, Abba, Father."

Romans 8:15

"Martha, tell Daddy that my car won't start."

"Mary, you call Daddy for everything. You don't give him a minute's rest."

"I do too give him rest. Now you tell him."

"Oh, Daddy," Mary said. "Martha's car won't start and you need to call her. But I took something out of the freezer to make for dinner tonight so you won't have to do that."

"OK, thank you, Martha. I declare, you are so reliable."

"Thank you, Daddy. I don't bother you all the time like somebody else we know."

"Now, now, you both are my daughters, and you are as different as day is to night. You both love me and I love the two of you."

"Let me show you a story in the Bible about two sisters with your same names. Turn in your Bible to Luke 10:38," he said and read the story of Mary and Martha.

"Now you can see clearly that the women were both loved. Both of their ministries were important to Jesus, but their callings were different. I have always taught you the importance of loving and having a caring and devoted family. I have loved both of you the same."

Where are you today in regards to your family? Are you estranged because of jealousy? Do you have a sibling that you dislike or distrust? Do you feel that a parent liked your sister or brother better? We serve a God that can eradicate the envy, the condemnation, and the root of bitterness that often accompanies family relationships. He can and he will restore to you the years that the canker worm and the palmer worm have eaten (Joel 2:25). He has a never failing, unconditional, restorative, agape love.

APPLICATION

Women of color, purchase some elegant stationery or a lovely card. Sit down and write to your family. Ask God to give you the words. Stick to positive things and write them down. A phone call is nice, but words to your sister or your brother on beautiful paper will indicate how much you care, and it will be something that she or he can always keep. Sometimes you have to read a note a few times before it really starts to sink in.

PRAYER

Most wise and reverent Lord God our Father, we thank you for family. It is so unfortunate that pain begets pain and hurt people hurt people. This pain and hurt occurs especially in family relationships. But, we thank you, God, that all things work together for the good of those that love you. Because of you, love begets love, and loved people, love people. Thank you for our families, God. In Jesus' name, Amen.

CAN I JUST LOVE EVERYBODY?

"But I have called you friends; for all things that I have heard of my Father I have made known to you."

John 15:15

"Oh my goodness, Hannah, I have not seen you since high school. What have you been doing with yourself, are you married?"

"No. I have been preaching the Word of God for about three years now. Speaking of God, how is your relationship with Jesus, Peninniah?"

"Oh girl, I know Jesus. What do you think, that I don't know Jesus? You're still not married, huh? Manasseh and I have been married six years already."

"Oh that is so nice Peninniah, how many children do you have?"

"Four."

"How are your parents, Peninniah?

"Both passed."

"I am sorry to hear that. Were they saved? Peninniah, if you should die tonight are you sure of where you would spend eternity? Do you have the children in Sunday school? Do you have a church home?"

"Look Hannah, I have to get home so that I can fix dinner. It was good seeing you."

The following Sunday as Hannah stood to preach, she saw Peninniah and her family sitting in a pew near the front!

We, the women of God and of color, have been given a mandate from God that we are to teach all nations, baptizing them in the name of the Father, and of the Son, and of the Holy Ghost. In everything, in every situation and in every relationship, we have a God to glorify.

APPLICATION

Women of color, never deny yourself the opportunity to point a friend to the cross. We cannot afford to miss those opportunities to be a part of the eternal destination of one of our friends. We are all so very busy most of the time, and sometimes we even get just a tad filled with ourselves. We sometimes fail to touch the hearts of the people that God has placed strategically in our lives. Give an old friend a call, and find out where she's at.

PRAYER

Lord, help us to be better friends. We will purpose that from this moment forward, we will strive toward loving everyone with the love of Christ. In Jesus' Name, Amen.

FEBRUARY

WEEK THREE: SOUL MATES

DAY 1 / WAITING FOR GOD

FINDING YOUR SOUL MATE FOR LIFE...

"But from the beginning of the creation God made them male and female. For this cause shall a man leave his father and mother, and cleave to his wife; And they twain shall be one flesh: so then they are no more twain, but one flesh. What therefore God hath joined together, let not man put asunder."

Mark 10:6-9

I remember it as if it was yesterday. I closed my eyes, and I prayed to the Father, "Now Lord, you don't really have to send him now, but please tell me, when will the man that you have for me come?"

Dare I rush God on such an important task? But, like so many sisters who saw age 30 right around the corner, I wondered what God was waiting for. Didn't God know about the biological clock that I felt was ticking away? Then I heard the Spirit of the Lord whisper softly in my ear that while I waited, he was not only preparing me for my soul mate, but also my mate for me.

Now, I can't attest to being a veteran of marriage. Lord knows that there are many that have tenure on me in this department, but I can truly say that I have a quality marriage with my soul mate, Willard, of close to nine years. Being a modern career couple, raising our four-year-old son can get hectic, but we have a rhythm that is special. I know without a shadow of a doubt that I married the man that God prepared for me. We have both learned what mature love feels like after all of these years because our love continues to grow deeper every day. I can truly say that Willard and I are best friends, and I feel blessed to share my life with such a focused, strong, responsible, and loving man.

The secret to a great marriage is to trust and honor your spouse. It is important that you bring 100 percent of you into the marriage in order to make it work. Even 99½ percent just won't do. Of course, your first love and commitment needs to be to our heavenly Father. Nothing should ever break that bond, not even marriage. God has to be at the head of your marriage. Without him, prepare for an extremely severe and bumpy ride.

APPLICATION

If you find yourself where I was 10 years ago, waiting on the Lord to send you your soul mate, be patient and know that if you truly pray to the Father and obey his Word, he will give you the desires of your heart. Being alone is part of the preparation phase. Feel comfortable in it. Use this time to grow in his Word.

If you are engaged, be sure to seek Christian counseling before taking the plunge. Marriage is not just about "warm fuzzies." Marriage is about responsibility and commitment and should never be taken lightly or entered into haphazardly.

PRAYER

Lord God Almighty, I pray for your matchless wisdom as you teach me the importance of patience and waiting. Father, keep my mind stayed on thee during this time in my life as I wait for that which you have prepared for me. Lord, I will put no other before you, as I want to grow deeper in your Word and learn to walk in your ways. Lord, I may not know what you have prepared for my future, but I will trust you, no matter what. In the name of Jesus I pray, Amen.

DAY 2 / SPIRITUAL LEADERSHIP IN MARRIAGE

HEADS AND SOUL MATES...

"Submitting yourselves one to another in the fear of God. Wives, submit yourselves unto your own husbands, as unto the Lord. For the husband is the head of the wife, even as Christ is the head of the church: and he is the saviour of the body. Therefore as the church is subject unto Christ, so let the wives be to their own husbands in every thing."

Ephesians 5:21-24

Submit in everything, Lord? Now, I'm not one to question what my Bible tells me, but you know how headstrong some of our sisters can be when it comes to submitting to...everything? There are many of us who feel that total submission is a far-outdated symbol of marriage and should not apply to today's couples. We sisters are doing our own thing professionally and academically. It's easy to see this way of thinking as archaic in the church and in society today. However, I beg to differ.

Now I'm no pushover—far from it. But I love that my husband leads my household. I'm comfortable and secure knowing that my man takes responsibility in this role. Don't get me wrong; we have our fair share of spats and disagreements, but when we reach gridlock, I'm comfortable with my role to submit. I'm an extremely successful senior vice-president/general manager of a gospel record label, but through the Word of God I clearly understand my role at home. It is not my desire to wear the pants in the family. I'm just not that insecure.

The wife submitting to her husband and respecting him as head does not mean, however, that the brothers can abuse this privilege by brutally demeaning their women. Paul has something to say about that, too!

APPLICATION

You hear all the time that "marriage is what you make it." Do your part to make your marriage work for you and not against you. Marriage is hard work, especially when your man has worked that last nerve! So the next time you feel a blowup coming, take a few deep breaths, step back, then step forward, and wrap your comforting arms around your husband and tell him that what you had planned to say doesn't really matter anymore. Then give him a big kiss and watch him melt in your arms.

PRAYER

Father, I pray for your loving protection over my marriage. Please give me the strength and wisdom to keep my place in my marriage. We will turn our troubles over to you because we know that you will never put anything more on us than we can bear. We trust your healing power during difficult times. In Jesus' name I pray, Amen.

DAY 3 / REFRESHING EACH OTHER IN MARRIAGE
ROMANCING YOUR SOUL MATE...

"Who can find a virtuous woman? for her price is far above rubies."
Proverbs 31:10

Life today for so many families is just plain hectic. Whether the wife works outside of the home or has the noble job of caring for the home front full time, there never seems to be enough time. Couples find themselves being pulled in so many directions that many lose sight of what brought them together in the first place. Many marriages today are being threatened because couples are so busy with work, raising children, and church commitments that many husbands and wives just don't—can't—find time for each other. Distance not only threatens the marriage but also may cause a serious breakdown in the overall family setting. Especially in today's times, we need strong families. Without them, our society will suffer.

APPLICATION

Romance is important in a marriage. Couples need to maintain a commitment to keeping the home fires burning. Work harder to not allow anything to threaten it. Ladies, we need to do our part to refresh our marriages, and here is what we all are going to do: First of all, light some scented candles (fragrance will light up any room). Next, put on some smooth jazz, and draw a warm bath. Need I say more? Do your thing, girlfriend, and make your husband feel like a king. After all, you are his queen. Take the time to enjoy each other and bring a little romance back into your marriage. You won't regret it.

PRAYER

Father God, I love my husband. Please stir up the love that you gave us so long ago. We bless and honor you, God, and we thank you for continuing to be the head of our marriage. We thank you for reminding us that our bond and commitment to each other is precious and should never be taken for granted. In Jesus name, Amen.

DAY 4 / DIFFERENT ROLES BUT SAME GOALS

SOUL MATES MOVE IN
THE SAME DIRECTION...

"And the Lord God caused a deep sleep to fall upon Adam and he slept:
and he took one of his ribs, and closed up the flesh instead thereof.
And the rib, which the Lord God had taken from man, made he a
woman, and brought her unto the man. And Adam said,
This is now bone of my bones, and flesh of my flesh:
she shall be called Woman, because she was taken out of Man."

Genesis 2:21-23

I remember in my childhood hearing the story of Adam and Eve in Sunday school and wondering how God could create life from another life. Today, the miracles of life still amaze me. When my son was born, holding him in my arms was overwhelming. As I looked into his eyes, then into my husband's eyes, I felt as if our earthly circle was now complete. My new role as mother became the single most important thing in life to me. My husband's role as father opened his eyes further to what life is and should be all about, and that is family. His most earnest pursuit at that time was to provide a solid foundation, build security, and lead a life that would be an example for his young son to follow.

It became clear to us that although we served in different roles as a family unit, our goals were the same: To build a Christ-led household and to raise our son in a home filled with lots of love.

Families must move in the same direction. It is time for the black family as a whole to come together. Outside negative influences on children will be less likely to penetrate if the children are raised in a loving and healthy home. No matter what kind of family it is—single mother, father, or grandparent—love should be the common denominator in all.

APPLICATION

If we would love on our children just a little tighter in their developmental years, then we would not lose so many of our sons and daughters to the streets.

PRAYER

Father God, help and strengthen our families. Give us families in which we all have the same goals, regardless of our different roles. We pray for the leaders of our households. May you encourage their hearts to build a solid foundation that is edifying. In Jesus' name I pray, Amen.

DAY 5 / THE PURPOSE OF MARRIAGE

WHEN IN DOUBT...

"And the Pharisees came to him, and asked him, Is it lawful for a man to put away his wife? tempting him. And he answered and said unto them, What did Moses command you? And they said, Moses suffered to write a bill of divorcement, and to put her away. And Jesus answered and said unto them, For the hardness of your heart he wrote you this precept. But from the beginning of the creation God made them male and female."

Mark 10:2-6

Back in the Bible days, you probably could have read story after story of infidelities that broke the marriage bond. Since the beginning of time, the marriage bond's sanctity has been attacked by outside influences. When you look at the present marriage scene, you see that there are many who don't take marriage seriously because they know that they can just go on "Divorce Court," air their dirty laundry in public, and be given that piece of paper that sets them free.

It is so sad that on a daily basis marriages are annulled and divorces have become commonplace. This is true both inside and outside of the church. Because it is so easy to divorce, people simply rush into marriage with strangers without the proper courtship and full knowledge of their beloved's background. Let's take a closer look at the person that we commit to spending our entire lives with!

APPLICATION

If you are contemplating marriage, really seek counseling and be prayerful about the decision. If the Lord does not send you the answer, affirming the person that you are planning to marry, ask again. When in doubt, just don't do it. The Bible speaks about the purpose of marriage. Study God's Word on this subject before you take the plunge.

PRAYER

God, grant me the wisdom to seek you as I contemplate taking my marriage vows. Lord God, help me to feel secure so that I won't rush into such an important decision. Lord, I want to feel your holy presence in my marriage-to-be. I will seek you, O God, before making this very important step. In Jesus' name I pray, Amen.

FEBRUARY

WEEK FOUR: LET'S TALK ABOUT SEX

DAY 1 / SEX-A ROMANTIC GIFT FROM GOD
ENJOY!

"Let thy fountain be blessed: and rejoice with the wife of thy youth. Let her be as the loving hind and pleasant roe; let her breasts satisfy thee at all times; and be thou ravished always with her love."
Proverbs 5: 18-19

Mary and Paul have been happily married for five years. In the beginning of their marriage sex was a major contributor to this happiness. Now, after five years, three cities called home and three beautiful children, Mary and Paul just can't seem to find time for each other or for sex. Whenever they do get an opportunity it's over in a flash, leaving Mary cold. Mary misses being satisfied, and she prays to God each night for him to grant her the courage to speak openly with Paul. She vaguely remembers those times when sex was great for her.

Mary decides to confide in her best friend, Carolyn, who has recently ended an extra-marital affair that she claims brought her and her husband closer. Carolyn tells Mary that she should consider finding another man to please her. "This new man will go out of his way to please you. Husbands just don't always embrace romance and foreplay." But Mary is committed to Paul and the last thing she wants to do is cheat on him.

God grants Mary the courage to break the silence, and she speaks to Paul about her needs and desires. Paul was unaware of how Mary felt. They both agree to make more time for each other and to openly communicate needs in all aspects of life. That night they took the kids to Paul's parents, had a wonderfully romantic dinner and time to make love. Afterward, they got on their knees, held hands, and gave praise to God.

God gave sex as a gift to married people for mutual enjoyment. Sex is a gift that was given to us not only for creation of life but also to be enjoyed. If your sex life with your husband is not on fire, ask God to grant you a match, take the initiative to light it, set it on fire, and keep God in your life to keep the fire burning.

APPLICATION

Today, ask yourself what's missing in your sex life. Send a prayer to the Lord asking for his strength of resolution. Remember, when prayers go up, blessings come down. Always understand that what is good to you is not always good for you. Listen to your heart and strive to do the right thing. Do not let nonbelievers steal your joy. Keep God first.

PRAYER

Lord, I understand that my sexual desires must be placed under your control so that I may find what I so desperately need. Give me the strength to be open and honest with my husband about this topic. Allow us to express the enjoyment of the gift you have given us. In the name of Jesus, I pray. Amen.

DAY 2 / A PART OF THE UNIQUE RELATIONSHIP OF MARRIAGE

ONLY AFTER MARRIAGE...

"For this is the will of God, even your sanctification, that ye should abstain from fornication: That every one of you should know how to possess his vessel in sanctification and honor."

1 Thessalonians 4:3,4

Cathy is unmarried and cannot understand why she continues to kiss frogs yet never finds a prince. She also has not been able to comprehend why breaking up with these frogs hurts so much. Cathy prays to the Lord daily, asking him to send that prince into her life.

One night after a breakup with a guy she had dated for more than a year, Cathy made a decision to stop asking the Lord to send her a prince but to ask him to help her become a better Christian. She had always known that sinning was much easier than doing what's right. Cathy realized that she would not hurt as much from the breakup with boyfriends if she had not sinned against her own body by engaging in premarital sex. Doing this had made her more susceptible to getting hurt. Cathy was giving a gift that could not be returned or exchanged.

The secret to great sex is that it must be the kind that is approved by the Lord. Sex is a gift from God and should be cherished like any precious gift. Saving yourself for your God-sent prince is the right thing to do. And for those of us that did not do that, just think of the hurt we created for ourselves. It really would not have hurt as much to break up with someone to whom you had not given everything.

APPLICATION

If you are not married, try to always remember that premarital sex can be destructive even when the effects are not immediately recognized. These effects can be both physical and emotional. They can be both reversible and irreversible. In today's world the effects from sex can kill.

PRAYER

Lord, help me to become a better Christian. Grant me self-control at all times. Help me to enjoy all the gifts that you have so gracefully given me. In the name of Jesus, I pray, Amen.

DAY 3 / FIND JOY IN YOUR OWN MATE

WHAT LOOKS GOOD TO YOU IS NOT ALWAYS GOOD FOR YOU...

"But I say unto you. That whosoever looketh on a woman to lust after her hath committed adultery with her already in his heart."
Matthew 5:28

Rosemary married the perfect guy. He was kind, educated, spiritual, successful, and handsome. The problem was that he had gained more than 30 pounds since their marriage 6 years ago. Rosemary was a personal trainer, and physical appearance was very important to her. She began to notice some of the guys at her gym and felt an attraction to them. Rosemary knew that she had a great husband, but she found that her sexual attraction for him had declined due to his weight gain. She had to ask God for support before she made a mistake.

Rosemary's husband, David, was very aware of his weight gain and was not very happy about it. His job required him to travel two weeks out of each month, and he attributed his weight gain to eating out at restaurants and not properly exercising. David sensed that his weight gain was a problem for Rosemary. He had even noticed his own inability to feel desirable.

One night Rosemary decided to play a game called, "Why my spouse married me." The purpose of this game was for both Rosemary and Paul to note the top 10 qualities each identified as critical to the other in making a decision to marry. Although physical attraction was not on her list, Rosemary found that Paul was very much aware of her need to have a fit man. Rosemary realized that her problem was Paul's problem as well. Through prayer and using her job skills, she developed an exercise plan and diet that would allow her husband to lose the extra pounds gained over the years.

When Rosemary presented the weight loss plan to him, he was grateful to God for giving her to him. He was glad that she had actually sensed that he was discontent with his weight and had taken the time to develop a way to help.

The Word says that love bears and endures all things. True love, with prayer and guidance from our Lord, can overcome all things. If the grass looks greener on the other side, put a little fertilizer on yours. Do not just complain, take action. Our Lord gives us the ability to initiate change.

APPLICATION

Take some time out with your mate and make a list of what you think he desires. Have him make a list of what he thinks you desire. Exchange lists. Compare his list to your personal list to see if he knows what you desire. He will do the same with the list you provide him. Come together in prayer once the lists have been compared. Work in the Lord to meet those desires.

PRAYER

Lord, I know I am not what I used to be and I am not what I ought to be. Give me the strength to understand what my spouse harbors in his heart. I come to you today asking that you forgive me for losing touch with my spouse and perhaps for beginning to look elsewhere. Help me to walk in the path of righteousness. In the name of Jesus, I pray, Amen.

DAY 4 / SEXUAL IMMORALITY
THE PRICE YOU PAY...

"And I say unto you, Whosoever shall put away his wife, except it be for fornication, and shall marry another, committeth adultery: and whoso marrieth her which is put away doth commit adultery."
Matthew 19:9

Sarah and David have only been married three months and have already begun to have problems. Sarah has remained close friends with several of her ex-boyfriends and finds herself occasionally talking with them about the problems in her marriage. She still believes that she married the right man and knows that David is a blessing sent by God.

One day while talking with one of her ex-boyfriends, they decided to meet at his apartment for lunch. Sarah and David had experienced the biggest fight of their marriage the night before, and she needed to talk to someone. One thing led to another and Sarah found herself doing more than just talking at this lunch meeting. Sarah felt horrible afterwards. They promised to never do it again and to not let anyone know what happened that day.

A few weeks later, Sarah found herself pregnant. She and David had received some counseling and things were better, but she now feared that she was not carrying David's child. Sarah had to tell David about her wrongdoing. David was devastated, but his love for the Lord and his love for Sarah and the unborn child did not allow him to leave her.

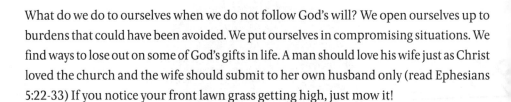

What do we do to ourselves when we do not follow God's will? We open ourselves up to burdens that could have been avoided. We put ourselves in compromising situations. We find ways to lose out on some of God's gifts in life. A man should love his wife just as Christ loved the church and the wife should submit to her own husband only (read Ephesians 5:22-33) If you notice your front lawn grass getting high, just mow it!

APPLICATION

Take some time today to examine how you discuss relationship disagreements with friends and family. Ask yourself if this is the right thing to do, especially if they will only hear your side. Friends and family do not always give good advice. Sometimes telling all of your business will allow for too much outside influence. If you must talk through your problems, find someone that will not take sides and that will offer Christian solutions. After an argument, try prayer. It changes things.

PRAYER

Lord, our Father who is in heaven, grant me the wisdom to accept the things I cannot change and to have truth, understanding, and courage to change the things I can. And I pray that you grant me the ability to know the difference. With your guidance, I can do better. I love you, Jesus, and in your name I ask for these things. Amen.

DAY 5 / WITHHOLDING AS PUNISHMENT

HE WON'T BE GETTING ANY TONIGHT!

"Defraud ye not one the other, except it be with consent for a time, that ye may give yourselves to fasting and prayer; and come together again, that Satan tempt you not for your incontinency."

1 Corinthians 7:5

Darlene is very mad at her husband, Raymond. How dare he not give her the money she needed for that new dress? She will fix him by putting him on the couch for the next week or two. It is extremely hard for Darlene to have sex with her husband when she is mad at him, even over petty issues.

Raymond gets very upset with Darlene's childish behavior. She once went a whole month without letting him touch her. Raymond loves Darlene and has always been faithful to her. But recently he found a friend in a young, single, female coworker and began to have lunch with her on occasion. During Darlene's withholding episodes, he found himself imagining more than just a friendly relationship with this coworker. Raymond knew that he loved Darlene and these thoughts were only circulating due to a physical need. He asked God to control these unwanted desires so that he would not give in to shameful lusts.

Hopefully there are lots of Raymond's in the world, but we all know that sometimes people will give in to their desires. Do not allow temptation to enter your marriage. The Word says that Satan will tempt you because of your lack of self-control. Try to satisfy your spouse. Do not withhold sex as a punishment. And never allow temptation of the body to enter your marriage.

APPLICATION

Ladies, let's not get crazy here. Our men have needs, and as a wife we should satisfy those needs when possible. Do not allow the other woman to enter your house because of your own selfish behavior. Marriage is give and take. Everything will not go your way all the time. Try to remember the last time you shared an intimate evening with your spouse. Plan a romantic evening and ask him out on a date.

PRAYER

Lord, I come to you today on bent knees, asking you to continue to bless my marriage. Give us the strength to continue to satisfy one another in a Christian way. Allow us to demonstrate our love for one another through our worship and actions. If I am angry, help me to find appropriate ways to work through it. I thank you, Lord, for all your blessings. In the name of Jesus, I pray. Amen.

CONTRIBUTORS

The Women of Color Daily Devotional

Montrie Rucker Adams

Dina Ruth Andrews

Cynthia D. Bellinger

Sonnie Beverly

Dr. Colleen Birchett

Mary Boston

Evelyn J. Curtiss

Anita A. Daniels

Robin M. Dial

Chandra Dixon

Jean Alicia Elster

Sharon Ewell Foster

Tammy Garnes

Portia George

Sha' Givens

Donna Green-Goodman

Rachelle Hollie Guillory

Tara Griggs-Magee

Sandra G. Gurley

Patricia Haley

Jan Hall-Lunn

Monique Headley

Michele Clark Jenkins

Winnie Sarah Clark Jenkins

Cathy Ann Johnson-Comforto

Kim Johnson

Jennifer Keitt

Marjorie Kimbrough

Jessica H. Love

Beverly Mahone

Regina Gail Malloy

Dolores E. Lee McCabe

Jaquelin S. McCord

Trevy A. McDonald

Jamel Meeks

Shawn Evans Mitchell

Norma Denise Mitchem

Charlene Price-Patterson

Linda Peavy

Rosalind Pollard

LaDena Renwick

Pamela L. Rollins

Catherine Ross

Vanessa R. Salami

Marlow Shields-Talton

Nicole B. Smith

Chandra SparkTaylor

Jacquelin Thomas

Karen L. Waddles

Marsha BrownWoodard

General Editor: Stephanie Perry Moore

NOTES

PEOPLE WHO MAY ALSO LIKE THIS BOOK:

....

....

....

....

....

....

NOTES

NOTES

LARGE PRINT

WOMEN *of* THE BIBLE
FOR
WOMEN *of* COLOR

$14.99
ISBN 978-0-9846480-5-4
51499>

9 780984 648054

PROMISES
FROM GOD
FOR
*Women of
Color*

$9.99
ISBN 978-0-9638127-1-1
50999>

9 780963 812711

GOALS

Become an US Urban Spirit! Publishing and Media Company
Independent or Church Distributor Today!

- earn extra money
- engage with more people
- change lives
- join a winning team
- distribute high-quality Bibles and books

Go to www.urbanspirit.biz

Order your Independent or Church Distributor
"Starter Kit" today online. It contains everything you need
to get started selling right away.
Or call **800.560.1690** to get started today!